DESIGNER
Genes

God Designed the Seeds
of Your Character
to Create Your Destiny

Ken Harrington

DESTINY IMAGE® PUBLISHERS, INC.
P.O. Box 310, Shippensburg, PA 17257-0310

"Speaking to the Purposes of God for this Generation and for the Generations to Come."

This book and all other Destiny Image, Revival Press, Mercy Place, Fresh Bread, Destiny Image Fiction, and Treasure House books are available at Christian bookstores and distributors worldwide.

For a U.S. bookstore nearest you, call 1-800-722-6774.
For more information on foreign distributors, call 717-532-3040.
Or reach us on the Internet: www.destinyimage.com

ISBN 10: 0-7684-2700-2
ISBN 13: 978-0-7684-2700-4

For Worldwide Distribution, Printed in the U.S.A.
1 2 3 4 5 6 7 8 9 10 11 / 12 11 10 09 08

Acknowledgments

"No man is an island, entire of itself; every man is a piece of the continent...."

—*John Donne,*
English clergyman and poet (1572-1631)[1]

No book is a product of one man's efforts or thoughts. It is in the combining of inspirations and talents that true genius is created. I would like to thank my dear wife and co-laborer, Jeanne Harrington, for her inspiration, support, and prophetic insights that made this book possible. She read and reread every page, was the impetus for most of the stories, corrected the details, and encouraged me when I went blank. Without her, there would be no book.

Thanks also to the tireless efforts of Brenda G. Smith, who did the initial editing, as I was writing, to make the thoughts palatable enough to even read.

As most of the earliest thoughts in this book were put down while I was still employed as an ironworker and before I had a laptop, I needed to have my "chicken scratches" transcribed. That job fell to the ladies of Spruce Grove Community Church. Thanks first to Myrna Mukli who organized and did the lion's share of the work. Thanks also to all those others who transcribed: Tangy Shields, Teresa Hunter, Suzanne Harrington, Laverne Kundert, Cheri Mitchell, and Shara-Rae Mitchell. Thanks also to Lauri MacKinnon for her photography.

I would also like to thank Destiny Image for taking a chance on this book. Special thanks to Don Nori, whose faith and enthusiasm prompted me to put my head down and finish this project. Also thanks to Ronda Ranalli for her wisdom in discerning the scope that this book should encompass and to Dean Drawbaugh for the efforts made to actually get it into print. Julie Martin also deserves much credit for doing the bulk of the editing. Her comments, which I admit were often irritating, forced me to take off the harsh edge, with which I often present ideas, and put forth a more readable book.

Most of all I acknowledge the inspiration of the Holy Spirit as being the true author of this book. I received the entire outline in a 45-minute period as He downloaded some of His desire for the Body of Christ in the area of character.

ENDNOTE

1. John Donne, *Meditation XVII,* http://www.online-literature.com/donne/409/.

Endorsements

Ken and Jeanne share lovingly from their hearts and from personal experiences about the essential principles of spiritual authority. This book should inspire many who desire to be more like Christ.

David Demian
Director, Watchmen for the Nations

We all want more authority and power in the spirit realm, but do we have the character to contain it? In this excellent book, Ken Harrington addresses this question and presents many practical insights and revelations from the Word of God and personal experience to bring the reader lower in the flesh but higher in the spirit.

Lorne and Rita Silverstein
Directors, Every Home for Jesus

The topics Ken and Jeanne cover in this book are vital areas of concern in ministry, both personally and for the many areas we deal with on the mission field. We have utilized their insight and expertise in ministering to prison inmates, recovering addicts in our street outreach, children in our orphanage, and our staff. It has brought freedom, liberty, and healing to their lives. We highly recommend this book and we will continue to use it regularly in every area of our ministry.

Every Christian needs to utilize the truths Ken and Jeanne share in this book!

Kim and Lynn Weiler
Fe Viva World Missions

In their own endearing style, Ken and Jeanne Harrington invite us to join them on their unique journey into Christ-likeness. They share honestly the battles and the triumphs, the failures and the victories, that work together to form in us godly character.

Along the way, you will pick up nuggets of gold and silver, precious stones, and pearls of wisdom. And if you pay close attention, you will also find "keys" that can unlock the mysteries of the Kingdom that you can put in your own treasure chest.

At the center of it all is the timeless and powerful challenge for us to "deny ourselves, take up our cross, and follow Jesus"—the mandate for every believer!

It has been my joy to know Ken and Jeanne now for many years. In all of our experiences together, I can truly say that they live what they proclaim. These pages do not merely present empty theories. These are truths that have been forged in the furnace of life. And now they are available to you! Enjoy!

Rev. Dennis Wiedrick
President, Wiedrick and Associates, Apostolic Ministries
Oshawa, Ontario

Table of Contents

Foreword

There is a difference between a man who speculates and one who does the work. Someone once said, "Those who can, *do*; those who can't, *teach*." Yet, there is another breed of people who "do" *and* "teach." When a person carries this combination of strengths, it brings a distinct kind of authority to the material being presented. This book represents that kind of combination.

A few years ago I came into a position of leadership in Spruce Grove. Like any other church there was an authority structure in place. However, I have discovered that not everyone who *has* a title *deserves* one. Thus I had one question. I did not need to know who were "deacons" or who were "elders."

My primary question was, "Lord, with whom do You speak concerning the future and direction of this Body?" This was not a question any man or woman could answer.

And so I waited, week after week. As I would pray and seek the counsel of God, I would watch for the ones who carried a similar word or burden. With great regularity, a couple who served as elders in the church would walk through my door. One week it would be a dream, the next it would be a testimony or a Scripture. Time after time, too often to be a coincidence, this same couple would bear the Word of the Lord. This was my answer!

Ken and Jeanne Harrington are a couple who walk the walk and talk the talk. Not only have they studied the Scriptures, they have applied them in such a way so as to validate their worthiness. I'm not saying we cannot just believe what is written. This we certainly can and should do. But there is something that happens deep within the heart of a man or woman who has believed, stood, and in the end is holding a verified outcome. This book represents not only Kingdom truths, but dozens and dozens of examples of how those truths are lived and apprehended by the average believer. In these chapters you will find beautiful gems and great nuggets of gold that have been hewn from the Mountain of God's Word. Enjoy each and every one of them!

Marc Brisebois
Senior Pastor, Spruce Grove Community Church
Director, Watchman on the Wall

Preface

This book has two main purposes:

1. To illustrate in a practical way the principles that allow an individual to walk in real authority.

2. To get the words of God, not just the principles, into people's spirits so that revelation, not just knowledge, can empower them.

To accomplish this, many Scriptures are interwoven throughout the text. I realize that many readers have a tendency to skip over Bible quotations in order to follow the flow of the author's ideas. However, I implore you to give God's Word the honor it is due. Read every word, and let it soak into your innermost being.

Jesus said, "All power is given unto Me in heaven and in earth" (Matt. 28:18). The Greek definition[1] of the word translated as "power" here implies authority, both the right and the might to perform an act.[2] Jesus wants to delegate that authority to His people on the earth. However, many of us have failed to understand that His authority comes out of His nature, not by force of will. This has created a situation where we have allowed mere might to masquerade as authority. When this type of might-based authority is exposed to pressure, it manifests its lack of character with disastrous results.

This book then is based upon the supposition that the authority (root word: *author*) rests in the Author or Creator of this world and will be manifested in us as He is allowed to be the author of the various aspects of our character. Thus, such concepts as forgiveness, love, humility, patience, joy, trust, faith, and hope are containers for this authority.

Through scriptural and personal examples and insights, this book will lead you, the reader, into a paradigm shift in the way you think about and access the power and authority in which God has destined you to walk.

ENDNOTES

1. George Ricker Berry, *Interlinear GREEK-ENGLISH New Testament* (Zondervan, 1973); and Spiros Zodhaites, *The Complete Word Study Dictionary: New Testament*, (Chattanooga, TN: AMG Publishers, 1992), #1849.

2. *Blue Letter Bible*, s.v. "Power," #1849.

Introduction

Does your life seem mundane and void of excitement and meaning? Have you ever felt that there was a hidden potential in you, but you couldn't get at it? God designed us to rise above the mundane plane of this world by laying hold of our destiny. Unfortunately, many of us don't even come close to our potential in Him.

We need to learn that *character is the key that opens the door to destiny*. Many gifted people have crashed on the rocks of life because their character could not sustain them, while people with less gifting, but great character, have come to places of prominence in the Body of Christ. It is my desire to see you come into the full potential of everything that God has designed for you to be. I wrote this book to give you keys to open the door of your destiny.

Gehazi was an apprentice prophet, in servant's robes, training to inherit the mantle of power that Elisha carried (see 2 Kings 4–5). Gehazi served Elisha and witnessed all the power and authority that he wielded. Elisha sent him to raise the dead, heal the sick, and to deliver his words. Gehazi even sat down with Elisha and discussed God's will for blessing people. He was destined to be God's prophetic voice, setting up and bringing down kings, but he had a character flaw; he was greedy.

Naaman, the Syrian captain, came to Elisha to get healed from leprosy. He was so thankful for his healing that he offered Elisha great wealth. Elisha refused to use the giftings of God for his own personal profit, but Gehazi was not so selfless; thus he erred in his decision to profit from the gift of healing that Elisha spoke over Naaman. That action revealed Gehazi's true nature; he held his own gain as more valuable than his service to Elisha or the inheritance of the prophet's office. Later in Scripture we find Gehazi relating the stories to the king of Israel about Elisha's miracles, rather than doing the miracles himself. Gehazi lost his destiny because he couldn't change the selfish way he thought.

To enable us to start that transformation, we must desire to walk in Jesus' character and not our own. This is our glory, which is *Christ in us* (see Col. 1:27). In a dream God gave me, I saw Jeanne and myself carrying armfuls of glowing balls. Each of these power balls had rays of light shooting out of them. I had so many balls that when one fell I couldn't even bend down to pick it up. God said these were spheres of authority. These spheres each represented different aspects of our character. Each characteristic—humility, faith, love, joy, etc.—is a container for God's power.

I had always assumed that power was resident in an individual like air in a balloon, all in one container in our spirit. I now understand that God has all the power and authority and it is resident in Jesus (see Matt. 28:18). As we allow Him to reside in the various areas of our character, His power will manifest itself through us to a hurting world. The door that will allow us access to real authority and power is our character—if it mirrors Christ's character. *Ultimately, the only enemy that can resist us in this battle is our own flesh.*

This is not a book on doctrine, though it does explain the principles of God's Kingdom. This is not a "how-to" book, though you will walk with Jeanne and me through our errors and victories. The purpose of this book is to impart life, Jesus' life, into your character and your spirit. This happens, like all other aspects of the Christian walk, through grace and faith (see Eph. 2:8). I have tried to be honest in the representation of my family's story. We are just ordinary people with an extraordinary God. We have experienced glory and shame in our lives. Both are profitable in God's hands to produce maturity and purity.

We will only come into our destiny if we allow God to refine our character. Gehazi didn't have the character to keep him where his calling would have taken him. His story and others are in the Bible for our sakes; "they are written for our admonition"

(1 Cor. 10:11), so that we might not follow their example but rather in Jesus' footsteps. Jesus said, "All things are possible to him who believes" (Mark 9:23). Therefore, "let us lay aside every weight, and the sin which doth so easily beset us, and let us run with patience the race that is set before us" (Heb. 12:1). We can do this, if we believe. Jesus has already run the race for us. He said He would carry us.

Observe our journey (my wife's and mine) in the pages of this book; it will encourage you in yours. *God enjoys transforming ordinary people into extraordinary conquerors by changing their character.* It is His greatest desire to see each of us becoming what He has created us to be. We will never be fulfilled unless we come into our destiny in Him. Through the pages of this book, I hope you are inspired to reach "for the prize of the high calling of God in Christ Jesus" (Phil. 3:14).

Chapter I

*Humble Yourself—***Humility**

Submission and Humility: the Low Door to Kingdom Authority

In our humanistic thoughts on humility and submission, we tend to relegate people who display these attributes to the lower levels of most power structures, but the Bible says that "the meek shall inherit the earth" (Ps. 37:11). In other words, when all the variables are played out and all the jostling for position is over, it is the meek who will be on the top as the inheritors (owners) of this planet and all its intricate systems. This is not what our thought processes would predict! If the ultimate authority will belong to the meek, then all who desire a place of prominence must choose to come *under* authority instead of pushing to *be* the authority.

God warns those who see their value as greater than others that they should be "clothed with humility, for 'God resists the proud, but gives grace to the humble'" (1 Pet. 5:5 NKJV). God actually puts roadblocks in the path of the proud but gives grace (unwarranted favor) to the humble.

Jeanne, my wife, learned this lesson early. She was a Brownie (a junior Girl Guide) when she was younger. Her troop was doing a project to bless a senior's lodge, and each of the girls was hoping to be the one chosen to present a fruit basket. All the little girls were excitedly jumping around, shouting, "Pick me! Pick me!" Jeanne was sure she would not be chosen, so she decided to clean up the mess the troop had made. However, as Jeanne was picking up papers and ribbons, the troop leader saw her and recognized that Jeanne was displaying the qualities that the Brownies were supposed to exemplify: humility and servanthood. Thus, Jeanne was chosen to present the gifts. That lesson has stayed with Jeanne all of her life and has allowed her to function in many high levels in the Kingdom.

The higher we are exalted, the more important it is for us to ignore the flatteries that others may give us. Most people only see us at our best. They aren't there when we are flipping out at the computer, or the leaky taps, or the kids. Charm is what we display for the outside world to see. We can act charming for a short period of time and put on a good façade, but like any act, it is not reality. Our character underlies the personality that we consistently walk in. We have to be able to laugh at ourselves and honestly admit that *our positions or titles in no way indicate the maturity of our character.* In fact, our positions often isolate us from the very circumstances that would mature us.

King Nebuchadnezzar was the most powerful leader the world had ever seen. His position prevented anyone from challenging his thoughts or ideas. He had absolute authority, made his subjects cower before him, and as a result, had become extremely proud.

The prophet Daniel humbly challenged King Nebuchadnezzar to recognize that it was God who "changes the times and the seasons; He removes kings and raises up kings" (Dan. 2:21 NKJV). The king ignored the warning. Not much later, Nebuchadnezzar had a prophetic dream in which a "watcher" (an angelic being) warned him that "the Most High rules in the kingdom of men, [and] gives it to whomever He will, and sets over it the lowest of men" (Dan. 4:17 NKJV).

The king failed to heed these two warnings and for a season had to be taught what it meant to be humbled by God. He actually went insane and began to *eat grass like an ox* (see Dan. 4:25). I think we could agree that it is preferable that we humble ourselves rather than waiting for God to do it for us. Jesus walked out this principle, and the Word challenges us to:

> *...let this mind be in you, which was also in Christ Jesus: who, being in the form of God...made Himself of no reputation, and took upon Him the form of a servant, and...humbled Himself.... Wherefore God also hath highly exalted Him, and given Him a name which is above every name* (Philippians 2:5-9).

23

God wants to exalt us, but too often He can't because we have too high an opinion of ourselves. Jesus highlighted this principle in a parable about a Pharisee who "stood and prayed thus with himself, God, I thank Thee, that I am not as other men are, extortioners, unjust, adulterers.... I fast twice in the week. I give tithes of all that I possess" (Luke 18:11-12). Meanwhile a publican "smote upon his breast, saying, God be merciful to me a sinner" (Luke 18:13). Jesus said, "I tell you, this man went down to his house justified...for every one that exalteth himself shall be abased; and he that humbleth himself shall be exalted" (Luke 18:14). God is much better at His job than I am at mine. I would rather humble myself and have Him exalt me than have it the other way around.

We have a friend, Drew, whom God called to carry a vision for a film studio that would be dedicated to producing Christian media. Drew proceeded to draw up a business plan and tried to bring this vision to pass. God said, "*Stop!* You're like a little locomotive pulling lots of baggage, and it is hard for you to stop at the station. Will you let Me kill you?" Drew, not knowing what this would entail, said, "Yes!" Thus began his journey through the desert.

Jeanne and I met Drew and his wife Julia about this time and wondered what was wrong with him. He had all this experience and potential but was doing nothing. He had good job offers, but chose to wait for his dream. Drew and Julia became stretched financially but always seemed to just make it.

God was trying to expose Drew's heart to Drew. Drew thought he was changing and dying to his old ways until one night he awoke with a terrifying pain in his chest and the overwhelming presence of a spirit hovering over his body. He felt pinned down to the bed and was prevented from even crying out. He was sure he was having a heart attack and was about to die. Horrified, he began to plead with the Lord, crying, "No, no, no! Not now, God, I have a wife and children. I can't leave. I want to be with them and teach them. And what about Mighty Motion Pictures? There's so much I have to do."

The Lord said, "See…you love your life."

Drew had to repent. "Lord, I'm sorry. My life isn't mine; it's Yours. If You want me now, take me. I'm Yours."

Instantly he could breathe again. Shortly after this experience, God elevated Drew and put him in charge of a multimillion-dollar production company.

Now, please don't misunderstand my reason for telling this story. I am not saying that we shouldn't ask God to heal us if we are stricken with an illness. However, in this case, God needed Drew to realize his utter dependence on Him and to respond by completely surrendering everything he loved, planned, and wished for.

We are all on a journey of humility and dependence. Our pride arises from our biased view of the things we do. We judge our value on the basis of our performance or our perceived performance. God's assessment comes from who we are and who we can be in Christ. The spread between these two always relates back to our character. *Our character will determine how far we can go in our calling.*

Suppose we were to use a scale from 1-10 for both our character and our calling. Ideally we would have both components at the same level. However, if our character is at a level 5 but our calling or anointing is designed for us to function at a level 7, we will be incapable of walking at that higher level. The pressures and exposure to higher levels of demonic attack, without a compensating level of character, would take us out. That is why high-level ministries often experience devastating moral failures: they don't have the character to match the calling. It would be more expedient for us to be demoted to function at a level 3 or 4 calling until God develops in us the level 7 character that is necessary to match the level 7 calling. This seeming demotion would kill our pride, and it is designed to do just that. That is how we develop higher levels of character: humble ourselves and die to those unredeemed areas of our flesh.

When I was much younger, I was informed that I was going to be laid off from a large job that was far from being finished. I was shocked. I was a Christian and should have been the last one laid off, not the first. My foreman, Stan, also a Christian, came to talk to me about what I had done wrong. It seemed that in my zeal to be a good witness for Christ, I had actually been a bad witness. My exhorting and teaching the guys I was working with had detracted from productivity. I just talked too much!

After Stan left, I had to humble myself and repent. I realized that true submission meant honoring the authority that God had placed over me and giving the company a full day's work for a full day's pay. I would have to witness on my own time, not the company's. Less than an hour later, Stan came back. He said, "I don't know what happened, but they want to transfer you over to the job on the other side of the lake. They want you to be a foreman over there."

I know what happened; I humbled myself. Do you want a higher position? Then take the lower position; humble yourself, repent, and God will exalt you.

During Jesus' time on earth, the Pharisees maintained an outward appearance of being the most righteous group, when it came to keeping the law. However, *keeping the law never develops character; it only develops pride.* Jesus' free spirit and character offended their legalism. Everybody but the Pharisees themselves could see their hypocrisy. Jesus called them "blind leaders of the blind" (Matt. 15:14). Their self-righteous pride prevented them from exercising proper judgment. These experts in the Scriptures could not recognize the Messiah because they were offended that Jesus manifested God outside of their box. Even Pilate knew that "for envy they [the Pharisees] had delivered Him [Jesus]" (Matt. 27:18). The keeping of the law had not touched their self-centeredness and self-importance. They were determined that their keeping of the law was the key issue because it established their authority.

*We do **not** have the ability to establish our own authority.* Once, when Jeanne and I were on our way to minister in Moose Jaw, Saskatchewan, Jeanne repeated a rash statement she had heard a speaker make on television. She mockingly cried, "Oh no, she's here!" We were joking about the demonic realm fearing our arrival. The problem was, the demonic realm wasn't afraid of us. For the next several hours, Jeanne suffered dizziness and nausea.

It wasn't until we realized our arrogance and repented of our pride that the symptoms went away. *Presumption is not power; presumption is not faith; it is sin.* God was gracious and did come through for us. We had a tremendous time of ministry, and there was much freedom and deliverance; but we learned that "power belongs to God" (Ps. 62:11 NKJV). It resides in God, not us. We had to operate in humility and submission if we wanted His authority to be manifested through us.

We are all subject to God's delineation of power. Jesus emphasized this to Pilate when He declared, "You could have no power at all against Me unless it had been given you from above" (John 19:11a NKJV). If we recognize the fact that all power is resident in God and that He is the arbitrator of who shall have it, we won't dispute, as the disciples did, about who is the greatest. They thought greatness was framed by abilities. Jesus corrected their misconceptions by expressing a different concept. He said, "He that is least among you all, the same shall be great" (Luke 9:48b). And "whosoever therefore shall humble himself as this little child, the same is greatest in the kingdom of heaven" (Matt. 18:4).

This was just the opposite of what they had witnessed in the world. The Kingdom of God is not like the kingdoms of this world. It has been called the upside-down kingdom because its laws are so contrary to the world's laws. Jesus said:

> ...*The princes* [rulers] *of the Gentiles exercise dominion over them, and they that are great exercise authority upon them. But it shall not be so among you: but whosoever will be great among you, let him be your minister;*

*and whosoever will be chief...let him be your servant:
Even as the Son of man came not to be ministered unto,
but to minister, and to give His life a ransom for many*
(Matthew 20:25-28).

***Our opinions are of no value unless they are in alignment
with Heaven's viewpoint.*** Otherwise we may find ourselves at
cross-purposes to what God is attempting to do in our lives.
"Humble yourselves therefore under the mighty hand of God,
that He may exalt you in due time" (1 Pet. 5:6). This advice flies
in the face of our natural bent to promote ourselves. We want
others to see us as of some reputation. God Himself is not worried about His reputation. In fact, Jesus "made Himself of no
reputation, and took...the form of a servant" (Phil. 2:7). Are we
willing to lay our reputations down? Can we play "second fiddle" to someone with less talent and maybe even less integrity?
Can we be the servant and help launch them into their destiny
in the Kingdom?

I once heard a sermon by E.C. Manning, a Canadian senator
and former Premier of the Province of Alberta, in which he
likened life to a baseball game. In this game of life, there were
two scoreboards. One was displaying hits and runs, indicating
to those in the stands who was winning. The other scoreboard
was unseen and displayed points, not on the basis of who scored
the most, but on the basis of who played the best (the player
who demonstrated the most loving, sportsmanlike conduct and
had the best attitude toward the other players, the umpires, the
coaches and the fans). As most of us have seen, if we watch any
sports, the scores on the two boards would not often reflect the

same victors. The challenge thrown out by Senator Manning was: Which game do you want to win? Whose approval do you really want? God's or the world's? It will have an impact on how we play the game.

Jesus was not interested in winning the game that was being played on earth. The outcome here did not affect His actions, as He explained to Pilate, who appeared to be the umpire of His fate. Jesus said, "My kingdom is not of this world. If My kingdom were of this world, My servants would fight...But now My kingdom is not from here" (John 18:36 NKJV). These dual kingdoms and scoreboards are very confusing to those who can't recognize any victor except the one on the world's scoreboard. Ultimately God's scoreboard will be the only one that matters when this world's game is dissolved.

We have a chance now to change our attitude and come into agreement with God, who "resists the proud, but gives grace to the humble." James goes on to say in that same passage, "...Submit to God. Resist the devil and he will flee from you" (James 4:6-7 NKJV). Submit and resist—that gains real authority. God has given each of us our own realm of authority. Authority could be defined as both the right and the might to do a task. Possessing that authority is dependent on our submission. We are not here to do our own will but the will of Him who bought us. We belong to God.

If we act according to God's will, He will grant us "power of attorney" over His resources. For example, if my company gives a lawyer this power, then the lawyer's name on a document carries the same legal weight as mine would. He would be able to enter into legally binding contracts or buy and sell items for which the company would be responsible. If the lawyer was to go beyond the scope of his responsibilities and start making decisions without prior authorization, he would be guilty of fraud. Similarly, we do not have "carte blanche" when it comes to exercising our authority. Even Jesus, when accused of doing things that the religious leaders thought were inappropriate, protested that He could "do nothing of Himself, but what He sees the Father do" (John 5:19 NKJV). He was submitted under the Father's authority.

I once listened to some good advice—not God's advice but good advice—on how to deal with a tax situation. I needed to borrow some money for a short period of time to do this transaction. Jeanne was not in agreement with my decision, but I was armed with this good advice so I ignored her. I went into a bank, and when the loan officer was off getting the papers, I felt something happen. The Holy Spirit had been dealing with me about this deal, and I suddenly realized that He was no longer there. I had been praying about this deal in my usual self-centered way: I would ask but not really wait for an answer. That way when I did what I wanted, I could say that I didn't disobey, I just didn't hear. Now I heard: "If you do this, you are on your own."

I should have gotten up and said, "I changed my mind." But I sat there. My pride was too big to admit I had been wrong, so I sat there, ruled by my pride. When the loan officer came back, I slavishly signed the papers and shuffled out. For the next three months we struggled financially. *There is no power without submission.* I could have learned by listening to the Spirit, but I chose to learn by going through the fire. Still, I did learn to hear the soft voice of the Spirit.

That situation was created by my sheer stupidity. At other times, satan will attack either through people or demonic powers. This is the bigger test. All hell may seem to be exercising pressure to cause us to step out of our place of authority. Adam came under this kind of attack in the Garden. He was offered authority (which he already had) if he would make a decision on a course of action, without submitting it to God. It cost him his relationship with God and all the authority he had. His descendants have suffered ever since.

Jesus also was under attack in a garden. All the forces of hell pressured Him. He was tempted to make a decision to do *His* will, not the Father's will. He was offered the possibility of not breaking His relationship with God and gaining all authority (which He already had) without the suffering. No wonder He sweated *blood* (see Luke 22:44). He chose not to exercise His own will but God's: "Not My will, but Yours, be done" (Luke 22:42 NKJV). This was in line with Jesus' own earlier teaching: "I tell you not to resist an evil person. But whoever slaps you on your right cheek, turn the other to him also" (Matt. 5:39 NKJV). In plain words, don't try to justify or protect yourself. If we don't feel covered or protected by someone else, we will automatically try to protect ourselves. This is part of our fleshly reaction of self-preservation.

The Lord is always challenging our normal worldview and exhorting us to shift to a Kingdom perspective and submit to God's plan for our lives. Jesus said, "Blessed are [you], when men shall revile you…persecute you…say all manner of evil against you falsely, for My sake. Rejoice, and be exceeding glad…" (Matt. 5:11-12). Why? "For great is your reward in heaven: for so persecuted they the prophets which were before you" (Matt. 5:12). This is part of our calling: to joyfully endure the attacks of the enemy. We are not to just suffer through this persecution; we are to seize it joyfully because of the reward God promises to us.

I once was employed as a superintendent to build a dragline, which is a huge, crane-like machine used in strip mining operations. Partway through the construction, the top management changed, and in the resulting struggle that ensued, I was replaced as superintendent. To me this felt like a demotion (and was), but God said, "Relax. I am in control." So I didn't fight or try to defend myself. With my new position of general foreman, I went from a salary structure to a wage based on hours worked. The extra hours I was working now became chargeable, and I earned $25,000 more than I would have had I not been "demoted." By submitting to God, I was able to allow Him to control my destiny.

When we try to protect ourselves, we are trying to control the situation. Control is always based on our fear of being out of control. If God is going to be in control, we must be out of control. Jesus said, "Let not your heart be troubled" (John 14:1). God knows our hearts; we don't! "The heart is deceitful above all things, and desperately wicked: who can know it?" (Jer. 17:9).

Victory over sin and our flesh should cause us joy, but we resist admitting that our hearts are wicked. We need to properly discern the state of our hearts before we can repent and get the victory. Humbling ourselves, in order to allow God to take control, is the key to having authority over our own flesh and to no longer be slaves to its demands.

Satan is our enemy, but his fifth column (his hidden or secret ally) is our flesh. Those rebellious areas in our flesh are where satan can reach down and get hooks in us. These are real places, actual realms of authority from which he can exercise his rule. Paul Keith Davis once related to me a vision in which he had seen 18 thrones in his soul. I had had a similar dream and was interested in discussing the dream with him. He related that to his surprise some of these thrones had demons seated on them. Those demons had access because those thrones (dominions) had not been placed under God's authority. Since all of what we are is supposed to be under God, our attempt to rule in those areas is an exercise of illegitimate authority. God said to me that these demon thrones were areas in me where satan had hooks.

Jesus had no areas where satan's hooks could grab because He had submitted all to the Holy Spirit in all His soul realms and could say "...the prince of this world cometh, and hath nothing [no place] in Me" (John 14:30). We need to get these areas in us healed so that they can be submitted to God's authority and be out of satan's reach.

Real authority comes because we are under authority. The centurion whom Jesus encountered recognized authority because he was functioning under authority. He announced, "I am...under authority, having soldiers under me" (Matt. 8:9). This centurion's authority came from the officers over him. The authority over us also establishes our authority. *If you have no authority over you, you have no authority at all.*

Wherever we allow illegitimate authority to function, it will always attract a demonic influence, as the vision concerning the 18 thrones demonstrated. Part of what God is doing is exposing those unsubmitted areas so we can repent and submit them to His authority. In the meantime we have to function in this carnal body which cannot humble itself. "The carnal mind…is not subject to the law of God, neither indeed can be. So then they that are in the flesh cannot please God" (Rom. 8:7-8). We need to humble ourselves and recognize that *there is no kingdom of self. Either we are submitted to the Kingdom of God or the kingdom of darkness.* Satan knows this and always attempts to pull us down to his level.

Positionally we "sit together in heavenly places in Christ Jesus" (Eph. 2:6). It is from the place of faith that we must fight. The taunt is to fight for your rights at a lower level, in the realm of this world. This was the last temptation that Jesus faced: "If You are the Son of God, come down from the cross" (Matt. 27:40 NKJV). In other words, "Come down (abandon Your proper realm), and claim Your rights in this realm." Jesus was too engaged in His Father's business to worry about what was happening to Him on the cross.

We, too, have a cross to bear. Jesus died for our souls; we must die to our souls. This means that we cannot be occupied with our status, reputation, or rights in this realm. Jesus has already defeated satan; we have authority and are seated with Christ. Satan knows this but will taunt us to come down to his level as he did Christ. He does this by accusation and lies. If we take offense (the Greek word for offense, *skandalon*, literally

35

means to take the bait-stick, which springs the trap[1]) and try to defend our name (reputation or rights), satan will win. Why? Because we are guilty of breaking the law just as he accuses us. The Bible says, "Whosoever shall keep the whole law, and yet offend in one point, he is guilty of all" (James 2:10). There is only one law. This law has ten links. You only have to break one link in a chain to break the chain. We all know we are guilty of sin. Satan simply accuses, true or not, to draw us out of our place of authority. It will be a vain attempt for us to try to defend that place by our own righteousness.

I will give an example. Suppose we have a sergeant in the army who is in charge of a group of new recruits. Now this sergeant is rather small, say 5'6" and about 160 pounds. Now suppose that a 6'4", 240-pound, belligerent recruit challenges him. If the sergeant stays in his place of authority, which is represented by the stripes on his uniform, he can draw on the full resources of the army, including MPs, to exercise his authority and make this recruit obey. But, if he gets offended and reacts to the recruit, saying as he takes off his uniform jacket, "Let's settle this behind the barracks," he has just stepped out of his position of authority. Now he is on his own and will likely take a beating. The recruit has power; the sergeant has authority. *We don't fight power with power. We fight power with authority.* Satan has more power than we have by ourselves because he can draw on the power of everybody who obeys him. However, we have authority that can draw on the power of Heaven, if we stay under the authority of Heaven. Jesus said that we are not to resist evil and that we should love our enemies (see Matt. 5:39,44). It is not our job to protect ourselves; it is His job.

The Bible gives us a couple of chapters with practical ways of how to avoid resisting evil and how to love our enemies (see Matt. 5–7). These instructions seem impossible unless we can trust God to cover us. I always thought these commands would make me a doormat and I would get run over if I acted according to Jesus' instructions. I had to remember that *humility or meekness is not weakness. It is strength under control, God's control.* Jesus says that the way to defeat satan's accusations is to humble ourselves and cast ourselves completely upon His ability to intercede for us. Therefore when satan accuses, "Agree with your adversary quickly…lest [he] deliver you to the judge…and you be thrown into prison" (Matt. 5:25 NKJV).

But God is the judge! Why would a just God throw us into prison? Because we are guilty! Satan is standing before a court in Heaven and is appealing to the law to say you did something wrong. You have two choices. Either you plead guilty and throw yourself on the mercy of the court, or you fight the accusation and plead not guilty, in which case there will be a trial. In the first scenario, the judge (God) takes your admission of guilt and humble response, in asking for mercy and grace, as a proper biblical response. "Come boldly unto the throne of grace, that we may obtain mercy, and find grace to help in time of need" (Heb. 4:16). When do we need mercy and grace? When we are guilty. Jesus paid the penalty for us already, and we can apply His blood to our guilt and, as far as the law is concerned, we can walk away free.

If we plead not guilty, then a second scenario unfolds. Satan appeals to the law and claims we did it wrong. If we protest, "No, I did it right," then we also are appealing to the law. If we choose this path then "Christ is become of no effect unto you, whosoever of you are justified by the law; [you] are fallen from grace" (Gal. 5:4). The law was not added to justify us but rather to convict us of our sin (see Gal. 3:19). Any attempt of ours to use the law will convict us. Therefore, the only way to maintain our authority, when satan accuses us, is to agree with him, repent to God, and fall on His mercy. We must let Jesus reap, or take the consequences of what we have been sowing in our flesh, in His body on the cross.

Jesus said, "Do not think I have come to destroy the Law.... I did not come to destroy but to fulfill" (Matt. 5:17 NKJV). Swallowing our pride and confessing our fault is humbling, but we know it is important since "God resists the proud, But gives grace to the humble" (James 4:6 NKJV). Satan wants us to use the power of our soul, our own flesh, to fight him because that will bring up our pride and we will end up fighting God, not him.

Jesus Himself "...learned obedience by the things which He suffered" (Heb. 5:8). This is a hard concept: Jesus the Son, though God, had to learn obedience. His Spirit was God but His body and soul were human. They had to learn to obey the Spirit just as ours do. He had to be 100 percent man if He was going to redeem man, because it was to man that God had given authority on the earth (see Gen. 1:28). "...Found in fashion as a man, He [Jesus] humbled Himself, and became obedient unto death, even the death of the cross" (Phil. 2:8).

There are two deaths mentioned here. Jesus died to Himself long before He went to the cross. He is our example. His willingness to die allowed God to exalt Him and give Him a name, which is above every name (see Phil. 2:9). We also must go this way of the cross. We must allow God to put us to death so that we can be "raised in glory [power]" (1 Cor. 15:43).

The way up is to allow God to take us down. We must give up control, yield it to God, and allow Him to mold us like a potter molds clay. We actually are clay. We were made from the dust of the earth. God wants to put His glory "in earthen vessels" (2 Cor. 4:7). God asks, "Cannot I do with you as this potter? ...Behold, as the clay is in the potter's hand, so are [you] in [My] hand" (Jer. 18:6).

The clay, to be flexible and moldable, must be worked and pounded to break the bonds that naturally hold it together. This working and bruising of the clay can be compared to the molding of our own hearts. God is not as concerned about our doing things right as He is about the condition of our hearts. Like the potter, God cannot work with a stubborn, hard heart of stiff clay but requires a pliable, bruised, or contrite heart. In fact, God looks for such people: "On this one will I look: on him who is poor and of a contrite spirit, and who trembles at My word" (Isa. 66:2 NKJV).

Before they had modern powders and makeup, ladies used to use a fine powder for a foundation called contrite or talc, which was made by grinding soapstone into dust. The word *contrite* means rubbed or bruised.[2] God loves "a broken and a contrite heart" (Ps. 51:17). My grandmother used contrite powder. When we were kids, we used to sneak into her bed-room, open the container, and blow on it. The contrite powder would cover the dresser top, and we could draw pictures in the dust that layered the surface.

God wants to engrave His image in us, so we must "fall on this stone [and] be broken…on whomsoever it shall fall, it will grind him to powder" (Matt. 21:44). As Christians we made a covenant with God to allow Him to form the image of His Son in us. He is going to keep His part of the bargain even if we try to back out because it was a covenant sealed in blood. Basically, Jesus is saying that there are two ways to become moldable: ei-ther we will bend and become broken, by our own volition, or He will make us contrite by His hand. God doesn't crush us be-cause He is angry with us but because He gave His word to us to make us "vessels of honor" (see 2 Tim. 2:21).

In the Book of Ezekiel God says, "I have wrought with you for My name's sake, not according to your wicked ways, nor according to your corrupt doings" (Ezek. 20:44). God made this covenant with Israel to prosper her in the land of Canaan, but because of the rebellion she sowed, she was reaping corruption. God had prophesied to Israel that the land itself would "Vomit you out…when you defile it, as it vomited out the nations that were before you" (Lev. 18:28 NKJV). As with a nation, so with a person; authority and power come as we submit to God's will. If we can't do what's right, then we must humble ourselves and come under grace. Otherwise we will find ourselves removed from the blessing and the promise of prosperity. It is a law.

So what does God do when we can't and won't do what is right? "I [God] sought for a man…that should make up the hedge, and stand in the gap before Me for the land, that I should not destroy it: but I found none" (Ezek. 22:30). God's heart was to forgive, but His justice demanded judgment. His solution was for an intercessor to carry the burden for the people. "If My people…shall humble themselves, and pray, and seek My face, and turn from their wicked ways; then will I hear from heaven, and will forgive their sin, and will heal their land" (2 Chron. 7:14).

God is not just talking about the dirt, but also about the relationships in the land. To properly intercede we must be able to identify with the group of people we are standing in the gap for.

Often when we pray or prophesy it comes out as accusation. If the people we are praying for were in the room, our prayers would often offend them. I remember being at a prayer meeting in a church where there was a lot of contention. One of the ladies prayed out, "Lord, make our pastor more loving and give him wisdom." I had coffee with the pastor and his wife afterward, and he was upset. His wife laughed and commented, "That was a good prayer. Isn't that what you want, to be more loving and to have wisdom?" Her husband shot back, "You know what she was saying. She was telling God and everyone else that I was unloving and stupid. That wasn't a prayer; it was an editorial."

To properly intercede, we must humble ourselves. How do we humble ourselves if, in our opinion, we have never done what we are praying about? For example, if we are crying out to God about murder in the land, but we ourselves have never participated in one, how can we humble ourselves in our experience?

The murder itself, like any other sinful action, is not the real problem; it is the fruit of the problem. The root cause lies deeper than the actions. Some of the roots of murder are: *revenge*, "I will make him pay for what he did to me"; monetary greed, "I will be better off if he is out of the picture"; *anger and unforgiveness, boiling up into hatred,* "The thought of her drives me crazy"; *fear*, "I thought he was going to hurt me"; *racism*, "You people are a blight on the earth"; and many more.

Have we ever done what was not right because of thoughts of revenge, money problems, anger and unforgiveness, fears, or racial prejudices? Of course we have. Then we can't say, "I don't know how they could do that." We know exactly why they did it because we have done many things for exactly the same reason. Once we have located the same sinful roots in ourselves, we can identify and humble ourselves in our experience and intercede as Daniel and Moses and Samuel did. They were all tempted in exactly the same way as those they were praying for (even if they didn't sin in the same way). Because they were willing to humble themselves, they had authority to deliver and heal. Likewise, our willingness to humble ourselves and intercede will break the power of the accuser.

God is calling us to bend our knees and acknowledge who we really are and what we really deserve. He wants to take us to a place where His blessing will be an indicator of our obedience, so we have the ability to correct our course.

Satan has attempted to delude us into believing that there is no God and there is no cursing or blessing in a situation. He wants us to believe that everything that happens is "just life." He doesn't want us to think that our actions even affect things like the weather. Satan wants us to believe that nature is only natural and is not affected by the supernatural.

When God took Israel into Canaan, He told them that things would be different. Even the way they grew crops would be different. He said, "The land which you [are going] to possess is not like the land of Egypt...where you sowed your seed and watered it by foot [irrigation wheels]" (Deut. 11:10 NKJV). No longer would self-effort get them prosperity. God wanted to tie their blessing in with their righteousness so He could bless them and correct them. "But the land...drinks water from the rain of heaven. ...If you earnestly obey My commandments...to love the Lord your God and serve Him with all your heart and with all your soul, then I will give you the rain for your land in its season" (Deut. 11:11,13-14 NKJV).

God wants us to be dependent on Him and wants our relationship with Him to determine our blessing so we won't become proud and independent. He had modeled it earlier for Israel in the wilderness. Moses reminded Israel that God humbled them to test them, and He allowed them to hunger, and He fed them with manna (see Deut. 8:2-3). Moses went on to warn them to keep the knowledge of the source of their supply in their remembrance, lest they should get proud and "say in thine heart, 'My power and the might of mine hand hath gotten me this wealth.' But thou shalt remember the Lord

43

thy God; for it is He that giveth thee power to get wealth..."
(Deut. 8:17-18).

Jesus emphasized this idea of dependence on God and His
desire for us to walk like He walked. However, to act like Jesus,
we must be able to think like Jesus. Jesus said of Himself, after
healing a lame man, "The Son can do nothing of Himself, but
what He sees the Father do" (John 5:19 NKJV). This dependence is a sign of true humility. Independence is a sign of pride.

Our independence often manifests itself in a similar manner
as the rich farmer's independence did in the story Jesus told.
The farmer in the story said to himself:

> *"What shall I do, because I have no room where to bestow*
> *my fruits? ...This will I do: I will pull down my barns,*
> *and build greater; and there will I bestow all my fruits*
> *and my goods. And I will say to my soul, Soul, thou hast*
> *much goods laid up for many years; take thine ease, eat,*
> *drink, and be merry." But God said unto him, "Thou*
> *fool, this night thy soul shall be required of thee"* (Luke
> 12:17-20).

There are 13 references to self—I, my, etc.—in just three
verses. "It's all about me." Even satan, in his rebellious declaration in Isaiah 14, only had five references to himself in two
verses. The farmer's arrogant declaration of independence
caused him to forfeit all that God had accumulated for him. God
had bent nature to bless this man.

Even Jesus, who as a man walked in greater authority than this
farmer, didn't attribute His authority to His own righteousness or

power. With this humble attitude, Jesus was
authority over the forces of nature and not to
anything spectacular. In fact, He often wondered at His o.
responses: "Why are you so fearful? How is it that you have no
faith?" (Mark 4:40 NKJV), but His disciples were in awe and
said, "What manner of man is this, that even the wind and the sea
obey Him?" (Mark 4:41).

He was a humble, submitted, obedient man just like we can be
through His power. Jesus did not come to demonstrate what God
could do but rather what a man could do submitted to God.

We must not think more highly of ourselves than we ought,
and we must not be wise in our own conceits (see Rom.
12:3,16). In fact, God has chosen the foolish things of the world
to confound the wise, the weak things to confound the mighty,
and the base things and despised things and things which are
not, God has chosen "to bring to nought things that are: That
no flesh should glory in His presence" (1 Cor. 1:28-29).

God wants us to exalt in Him not ourselves, "[You are] in
Christ Jesus, who of God is made unto us wisdom, and righteousness, and sanctification, and redemption.... He that [glo-
ries], let him glory in the Lord" (1 Cor. 1:30-31).

We are often like children helping their father lift a heavy
item. Just because they put some effort into lifting, they think
they "helped." We are told to put no confidence in the flesh. It actually doesn't help. The flesh is always trying to earn its way into
acceptance. Some people only help so as to create a debt they can
demand a return on later; that is not love. God gave in love. We are

45

not saved because of debt, but by grace (unwarranted, unearned favor) "through faith; and that not of yourselves: it is the gift of God: not of works, lest any man should boast" (Eph. 2:8-9).

We must unlearn our notion that we must work for what we get. Jeanne and I have some friends to whom God had been teaching this principle. They had not been raised in strongly supportive families. This had created a thought pattern in them that whatever they needed, they would have to supply for themselves. God, however, was about to smash that stronghold.

They had a small old house in Edmonton but wanted to move just outside the city to where their church was located. They agonized over whether to buy used or to build a new house. God prompted them to build even though this seemed extravagant and would put them back into a mortgage. They locked in the price with a contractor and started to build. Things took longer than expected because labor was at a premium, and they were unable to move in for many months. This problem turned into a blessing. During the time they were stuck with their old house, prices skyrocketed. The value of their old house increased so much that by the time they moved they had exchanged a small, old, $160,000 house for a brand-new, huge, $585,000 house. The dreaded mortgage was not even required. They owed zero! That $425,000 increase they accumulated was not gained by effort or sound financial reasoning. It was the blessing God used to change their way of thinking.

We can't save ourselves. Neither can we cause ourselves to grow or change. I have said many times, "I'll do better; I'll change," but the truth is, I can't. "Can the Ethiopian change his skin, or the leopard his spots? then may [you] also do good, that are accustomed to do evil" (Jer. 13:23).

The answer is no. That is a humbling fact that only Jesus has an answer for. Change does not happen through our striving or even our awareness of our weakness. It is not accomplished by mental gymnastics or positive thinking; as Jesus pointed out, "And which of you with taking thought can add to his stature one cubit? If ye then be not able to do that thing which is least [the physical change], why take ye thought for the rest [the inner man]?" (Luke 12:25-26). Jesus is talking about exchanging the glory we have as people for the glory He has as God. We can't work for His glory. He has to clothe us.

> *Consider the lilies how they grow: they toil not, they spin not; and yet I say unto you, that Solomon in all his glory was not* [clothed] *like one of these. If then God so clothe the grass...how much more will He clothe you, Oh ye of little faith? ...Seek ye the kingdom of God; and all these things shall be added unto you* (Luke 12:27-28,31).

Prosperity is not the sign of authority with God. If we think this, then we are "proud, knowing nothing...supposing that gain is godliness" (1 Tim. 6:4-5). But gain (prosperity) will reflect the condition (growth) of our souls: "that you may prosper...and be in health, just as your soul prospers" (3 John 2 NKJV).

If we understand that "...all things come of Thee [God], and of Thine own have we given Thee" (1 Chron. 29:14), then we won't be proud of our prosperity and we can freely use it as God directs, both for the Kingdom and ourselves.

This acknowledgment of God as our provider is hard on some people. I remember being asked to pray before a meal and bless the food. The man of the house got very angry because I thanked God for supplying the food. In his opinion, he had worked for the food and was not about to acknowledge that God had anything to do with it. He just wanted God to bless what he had done. The flesh is very proud of its accomplishments.

Humbling of the flesh and the soul will cause you to suffer because the flesh of its own accord cannot be "subject to the law of God" (Rom. 8:7). The soul (will, intellect, and emotions) must also give up its preeminence, which will cause it no end of grief. This suffering is not designed to be permanent any more than Christ was called to suffer: "*Not* that He should offer Himself *often*...but now, *once* at the end of the ages, He has appeared to put away sin by the sacrifice of Himself. ...Christ was offered *once* to bear the sins of many" (Heb. 9:25-26,28 NKJV).

The humility of suffering is designed to *kill*, not to maim. God does not want to hurt us or fix us; He wants to destroy us (our self life). No matter how we try, we need help to drive that last spike into our own "cross." But, as I am sure you have noticed, there are lots of candidates who are willing to help you suffer by driving in that spike for you. And God is willing to let them help. The question is, are we? Can we play "second fiddle" to a perceived poorer first violin? Are we more interested in advancing others or ourselves? If we would judge others, not on the basis of what we do well, but rather on what we do poorly, then we could not think of ourselves more highly than we ought to think, and we could, in humility of mind, esteem others as better than ourselves (see Rom. 12:3; Phil. 2:3). Our posture, if we are dead to our own ambition, will be a willingness to stay hidden until the Father wants us to be seen. This is true death that will end up in true life.

If we understand that death must precede resurrection and new life, then we can understand when the Scripture says, "If we be dead with Him, we shall also live with Him: if we suffer, we shall also reign with Him..." (2 Tim. 2:11-12). It is when we reign that we rule and have authority. This is God's whole purpose for our sufferings; it is not an imposed purgatory but the gateway to power.

When I was a young Christian, God took me through an interesting experience. I ended up with a wrenched back. I had to ratchet myself down to bend over and ratchet myself back up to stand. There was no comfortable position. We were having a prayer meeting one night, and I asked a friend to pray for me. He didn't have any faith, so we had to pray for his unbelief before he would pray for my healing. We were a powerful bunch! He prayed for me, and the meeting ended. The next day I went to work, but my back was still sore. I had believed that I would be healed, and later, after work, I questioned God on why I wasn't. He asked me, "When people at work asked you how your back felt, what was your reply?"

"I told them that it was bad."

"That is your problem," God replied.

He left me to ponder my next move. I realized that God was looking for me to claim my healing, not just ask for it. I had to participate in it. Then God asked another question: "What are you going to say about your back tomorrow?"

I started to review the next day's scenario in my mind. I can hardly move, but I am claiming I am healed. That will make me look brilliant. Finally God had me where He wanted me: ready for death, the death to my pride. I could have my pride, or I could have my healing. I chose healing. I was willing to look like a fool, a proper religious fanatic, claiming my healing and unable to barely move. I went to sleep knowing what I had to do. In the morning, I woke up and was completely healed. The death had been accomplished in private; I didn't have to walk it out publicly, just willingly.

This is why God calls us to rejoice when we are partakers of Christ's sufferings. If we are reproached for the name of Christ, He calls us "happy" because the spirit of glory and of God rests on us (see 1 Pet. 4:13-14). If we want the glory, we must be willing to go through what God knows we need in order to obtain it. God actually lays out a formula to come into His favor: "If when you do what is right and suffer for it you patiently endure it, this finds favor with God" (1 Pet. 2:20 NASB). So what do we have here? Doing what is right (taking your responsibility), suffering for it (not getting a right response), and patiently enduring (relaxing or resting).

> *FORMULA: RESPONSIBILITY – OUR RIGHTS + REST (OR PATIENCE) = FAVOR WITH GOD*

It is the "minus our rights" part that is often so hard. I switched from building draglines to maintaining them. For some reason, this caused problems when I joined the union at the mine. They hated me. I had my tools stolen, my coveralls filled with grease, and constant grievances filed against me. God told me to keep my mouth shut and He would vindicate me. Finally the union brought in a lawyer to see if they could oust me. A special meeting was called, and I was summoned to appear. This was all so bizarre because usually it is the company trying to turf the worker and the union trying to protect his job, not the other way around.

A whole bunch of accusations were thrown around that I wasn't qualified, I had no education, I had no experience, and that somebody should bump me with more seniority (who likewise would not be qualified). The mood at the meeting was ugly. Then it was my turn to speak.

I simply laid out my qualifications and experience. I added that as a union brother they should be concerned about my job and not just be in such a hurry to cash my dues checks. Then I sat down, and the strangest thing happened. They all started to clap and cheer, and the meeting ended. People came up and congratulated me and shook my hand. All the persecution stopped. From that time forward, God gave me great favor to share my testimony and allow me to speak into their lives and bring many to the Lord. My stance of humility and patience as I kept doing my job allowed God to give me favor.

Favor is better than position. For example, in elementary school, if you were the teacher's pet, you didn't have to be the smartest to get the privileges. If you have favor with the boss, you don't have to work the hardest or be the most productive to get the promotion. In fact, you don't even have to have position to get the perks, especially if you are the boss's son. In this Western culture, nepotism is frowned upon, but in the Eastern culture, which is the culture of the Bible, it is considered an obligation. Those who didn't show favor to son and daughter, nieces and nephews and brother-in-laws, would be considered like a heathen.

God's kids get favor. Take the prophets, "for an example of suffering affliction, and of patience. ...We count them happy [blessed] which endure" (James 5:10-11). These were ordinary men who had authority and power, and so can we if we follow the same paths they did. They knew God as a Father who loved them. God is the author of nepotism. He chooses His children's callings on the basis of their heart attitude. The humble heart that submits to God's choice will be exalted.

That is why a choice was made between Jacob and Esau:

- *Not on the basis of position.* Traditionally, the elder son was to be preeminent, but God made the choice that "the elder shall serve the younger" (Rom. 9:12);

- *Not on the basis of works.* "The children not yet being born, nor having done any good or evil...not of works, but of Him who calls [election]" (Rom. 9:11 NKJV);

- *Not on the basis of will.* "So then it does not depend on the man who wills [wants]...or the man who runs [works], but on God who has mercy" (Rom. 9:16 NASB).

- ***Rather according to His purposes.*** "For the Scripture says to Pharaoh, 'For this very purpose I raised you up [gave you power], to demonstrate My power in you, and that My name be proclaimed throughout the whole earth" (Rom. 9:17 NASB).

Therefore if we want to have God's purposes fulfilled in us, we must humble ourselves and come under His submission principle (equation): Responsibility – Rights + Patience = Favor. In His primary relational structure, the family, this principle is to be first worked out. Jeanne cried when she found out that she was to submit to me. However, as God trained her, she found that she enjoyed the favor God gave her as she submitted.

Jeanne calls it the Sarah/Abraham covenant. Sarah submitted to Abraham's ridiculous demand that she should say, "He [Abraham] is my brother" (Gen. 20:13). This statement got her put in a harem not once but twice. In the short run, her submission didn't seem to bring her into a place of favor but rather disaster. God, however, was working things out in her and for her. He closed all the wombs in Abimelech's household so that none of the women—his wife and female servants—got pregnant. Now it wouldn't be apparent in just a month or two that nobody is getting pregnant, so we can deduce that Sarah was in the harem for a long time, but God protected her. God finally came in a dream to King Abimelech and threatened him with death if he didn't let her go. Abimelech gave Abraham gifts and money and vindicated Sarah (see Gen. 20).

Sarah must not have been very pleased with Abraham for letting her take the heat to save his skin, yet she "obeyed Abraham, calling him lord, and you have become her children if you do what is right without being frightened by any fear" (1 Pet. 3:6 NASB). She received protection and opened the door of authority for Abraham to heal King Abimelech's household from barrenness. Sarah herself, at 90 years old, also received strength to conceive.

Israel as a nation had to submit, just as Sarah did, to God's instrument of judgment: the King of Babylon. God said to Israel, "Bring your necks under the yoke of the king of Babylon, and serve him...and live. ...After seventy years...I will visit you, and perform My good word toward you.... For I know the thoughts that I think toward you...thoughts of peace, and not of evil, to give you an expected end" (Jer. 27:12; 29:10-11).

Those who would not humble themselves and give up their nation died. Those who did come "under the yoke" lived (see Jer. 27:12). God was preparing the nation to receive greater things (the Messiah). The Babylonian captivity was designed to cleanse Israel of idolatry.

The captivity of Israel was a time of forced submission under Babylon. God had intended that they submit under Him with a trusting heart, but they were not willing. As a result, they *had* to submit—though they never humbled themselves. As soon as the punishment was over, they returned to their former ways. They forgot the lesson or even the fact that there had been any correction. Even the Jews in Jesus' time refused to remember their bondages and therefore couldn't learn from their experiences. Jesus challenged them to know the truth and be free, but the Jews replied, "We [are] Abraham's seed, and were never in bondage" (John 8:33).

They had been 400 years in Egypt, 70 years in Babylon, now were under Roman occupation; yet they claimed they were never in bondage. Pride will always blind us so we can't see what is right in front of our faces. Humility gives us right perspective on the truth—the truth about our situations and the truth about ourselves. Our goal in learning submission is to recognize that "there is no power but of God: [and] the powers that be are ordained of God" (Rom. 13:1). Therefore you need to "be subject, not only for wrath, but for conscience sake" (Rom. 13:5). Our conscience is one of the functions of our spirit. If our spirit is awake and working, we will not just be able to repent when we do something wrong; we will be able to detect ahead of time when an action will hurt God or someone else and humbly resist that particular urging of the flesh.

Humbling ourselves is one of the steps required if we are going to walk in the spirit. Resisting in pride is an indication that we are actually walking in the flesh. We are God's servants, and we need to act like it. Our circumstances should not dictate the function of our conscience. Our circumstances should not dictate our liberty for "he that is called…being a servant, is the Lord's freeman: likewise also he that is called, being free, is Christ's servant" (1 Cor. 7:22). We are not bound by our circumstances, but we are bondservants to Christ. Bound up in love, we are free to be "subject to principalities and powers, to obey magistrates" (Titus 3:1).

This attitude of freedom in submission must be in us if we are going to fulfill God's calling. First John 4:20 declares that we can't love God whom we can't see, if we can't love those whom we can see. It follows, then, that we can't obey God whom we can't see, if we can't obey those over us who we can see. Jesus could totally submit to the evil authority trying to destroy Him because He was actually submitting to God—to whom those evil powers had to answer. This requires great humility and an end of self-will. Jesus' submission won the greatest victory ever and regained our authority and freedom for us.

We also can set others free by humbling ourselves. Fasting God's way is one way of setting others free.

> *Is this not the fast that I* [God] *have chosen: To loose the bonds of wickedness, to undo the heavy burdens, to let the oppressed go free, and that you break every yoke? …Then your light shall break forth…your healing shall spring forth speedily, and your righteousness shall go before you; the glory of the Lord shall be your rear guard* (Isa. 58:6,8 NKJV).

Now that's authority and power! This act of humbling our flesh for others, laying down our lives for others, is the highest form of love. This action releases God to act on our behalf because He says that He "gives grace [favor]…to the humble" (Prov. 3:34 NKJV).

We are not our own; we are bought with a price, not to be slaves but to be joint heirs with Christ. The way to this high road of God is the low road of humility. The parable about the seating arrangements at the feast was an urging by Jesus for His disciples to take the lower seats, for "whoever exalts himself will be humbled, and he who humbles himself will be exalted" (Luke 14:11 NKJV). God wants to exalt us, and it is His "good pleasure to give you the kingdom" (Luke 12:32); but He can't if we won't humble ourselves first. One of the containers for God's power and authority is our humility. Jesus walked in it; so can we.

ENDNOTES

1. James Strong, *The New Strong's Expanded Exhaustive Concordance of the Bible* (Nashville, TN: Thomas Nelson, 2001); "Greek Dictionary," *skandalon*, number 4625.

2. *Webster's New Twentieth Century Dictionary*, s.v. "Contrite."

Chapter 2

Walking on Water—Faith

Faith is the language that Heaven uses to bring Heaven to earth. We read in the Word, "Death and life are in the power of the tongue" (Prov. 18:21), yet we must not believe it. If we did, we would not say many of the things that we do, such as:

- "I'm so sick and tired of…"

- "You just kill me…"

- "I hate this job…"

- "This headache is killing me…"

- "I'm so stupid…"

We often say these and many other similar expressions, which are actually word curses. We justify our negative speech, exclaiming that they are just expressions and don't really mean anything. Such glib statements take on much more meaning when a person in authority speaks them. The words "I hate you," if screamed by a three-year-old, don't carry the same weight for a mother as it would if her husband said it. A construction worker may declare, "I think the Americans should get out of Iraq," and nobody will take note. If the Prime Minister of Canada said that, there would be an international incident. Why the different responses, even though both parties said the same thing? The reason is that one has more authority, and his words, as the head of the government, indicate policy. The construction worker has virtually no authority in the country; therefore what he thinks is of minor consequence.

In your own life, you are the absolute authority. You sit as king or queen over your own personal realm. Nobody can compel or coerce you into adopting their point of view. God Himself will not violate the boundaries of your kingdom. He declared, "Behold I stand at the door, and knock: if any man hear my voice, and open the door, I will come in" (Rev. 3:20). Satan and people may try to cross your boundaries, but God won't. Jesus is a gentleman and does not push but waits to be invited into those areas that He has assigned to our stewardship. God gave the earth to the "children of men" (see Ps. 115:16), and He is still using man as the authority on earth (see Gen. 1:28). That is why Jesus had to come as a man so that He would have authority here by reason of origin. Paul spoke about the metron or measure of his rule or realm of authority or the boundaries within which he was allowed to function.[1] That realm, or measure of rule (see 2 Cor. 4:13), was his portion of the earth that God made him ruler over. Even the ocean was given boundaries and commanded to operate within them (see Job 38:11). Respect for our boundaries is one of the ways that we can determine if something is from God or not.

God has given us a realm of authority in the earth and appointed us as absolute sovereigns within our own lives. He has created us in His image to function like Him (ideally under His covering). We must exercise faith so that our words, repeating His words, carry weight and activate either demons or angels to carry them out. This may sound bizarre, but the Bible is clear: "A fool's mouth is his destruction, and his lips are the snare of his soul" (Prov. 18:7). The opposite is also true: "A wholesome tongue is a tree of life" (Prov. 15:4). James says, "The tongue is a little member...[and is a] fire. ...It [defiles] the whole body and [sets] on fire the course of nature, and it is set on fire of hell" (James 3:5-6).

These are strong words concerning such a small member. The tongue is, however, just the messenger. After all, it is "out of the abundance of the heart [the] mouth speaks" (Luke 6:45 NKJV). It is our heart that is the seat of our character, and it is the heart that God looks at. We don't actually know our own heart. God is aware that "the heart is deceitful above all things, and desperately wicked: who can know it? I the Lord search the heart, I try the reins, even to give every man according to his ways, and according to the fruit of his doings" (Jer. 17:9-10). Our mouth is the only real indicator of what we have in our hearts. The words are the fruit that indicate the roots hidden in our hearts.

God judges our fruitfulness, not our potential, not our faithfulness. Promotion comes from fruitfulness; we grow in areas of our fruitfulness. The parable of the talents reveals this particular law of the Kingdom of God. The king rebuked the servant who didn't produce anything with his one talent and commands that they take his talent from him and "give it to him who has ten talents. 'For to everyone who has, more will be given, and he will have abundance'" (Matt. 25:28-29 NKJV). God rewards fruitfulness! The wicked servant in the same parable had demonstrated what was in his heart by speaking poorly of the king. He said, essentially, "I feared you because you are an austere man: you take up what you didn't lay down and reap what you didn't sow" (see Luke 19:21). In other words, "You're hard, harsh, and a thief." That was a foolish thing to say to his boss, but it was what was in his heart.

We should "...offer the sacrifice of praise to God continually, that is, the fruit of our lips giving thanks to His name" (Heb. 13:15), but if our hearts are unthankful, our mouths will speak that eventually. The heart and the mouth are intertwined. That connection is the key to everything we get from God. Jeanne and I have learned this principle, so we have determined to declare that God is good. It has become part of our character to believe that everything He does is good and that we can trust Him. To speak the opposite would be to enact the opposite. The Book of Romans says, "If you confess with your mouth the Lord Jesus and believe in your heart that God has raised Him from the dead, you will be saved. For with the heart one believes unto righteousness, and with the mouth confession is made unto salvation" (Rom. 10:9-10 NKJV). This is the process by which we enter the Kingdom of God. This is salvation. We hear God, we believe, and we declare what we believe. This is the primary activating process that functions in every realm of God's Kingdom. We use this process: hearing, believing, and declaring to access healing, finances, deliverance, or anything else we want to activate; this is faith.

The Bible says that "faith comes by hearing, and hearing by the word of God" (Rom. 10:17 NKJV). This is how God says His faith works. First, we have to hear a word from God. This can come in innumerable ways: the Bible, prayer, a prophetic word, somebody saying something that catches your attention, the radio, a book, a movie, a bird on a tree. Anything can be a vehicle for God's word. Second, we have to believe with all our heart what God has said. This is more than mental assent; it is the knowing in our spirits that what God said is true. Third, we must declare into our realm of authority what we believe.

This faith response will move the mountains in our lives. However, we must say what we believe, not just think it. "Whosoever shall say…and shall not doubt in his heart, but shall believe that those things which he [said] shall come to pass; he shall have whatsoever he [says]" (Mark 11:23). Now that is power! The problem is that most of the time we can't seem to master this power because we can't master our mouths (see James 3:8). Part of the problem is that we really don't believe or don't believe the right thing.

Mark goes on to say, "Believe that you receive them, and you will have them" (Mark 11:24 NKJV). What are we to believe? Believe that we receive! My own personal problem was believing.

I couldn't believe for my healing if I still felt sick. I needed a manifestation to believe or I wasn't healed. What I needed to believe was that I received what I asked for. I need to say that again. The difference is subtle but profound. I believe to receive; not I believe the healing, but I believe the receiving: "Believe that ye receive...and ye shall have" (Mark 11:24). If I believe it, then I declare, "I receive." It is the declaration of receiving that settles the deal; the healing will follow. "These signs shall follow them that believe" (Mark 16:17).

Jeanne and I have bought and sold many properties in our lives. Every one of those transactions had a "subject to" clause attached to the sale. It might be: subject to financing, subject to inspection, subject to repairing the furnace, etc. The sale was not final until these "subject to" clauses were removed. It is the same with the faith agreement. Unless we remove our "subject to conditions," the transaction will not be completed and we will not get what we want. We can have a clause that says: subject to my feeling that I received, subject to seeing some results, subject to some timeline or whatever. Remove those "subject to's"; close the deal. Say, "I'll take it. I receive."

Satan tries to get us to rationalize what the Word says. We tend to adjust our doctrine to our experience instead of the other way around. We also hear what we want to. If we don't like what we hear from God, then we just ignore Him. We state what our thoughts are about a situation. This is presumption. We use presumption when we feel we have to be in control.

I used to do this all the time. I would pray, knowing what God thought on a matter but still wanting what I wanted.

Jeanne would ask me what God had said, and I would go through some vague explanation of what I thought. That was my ruse. Then I would just go and do it my way. That is presumption. *Presumption* is defined as acting highhandedly or proudly. There is no sacrifice in the Old Testament for the sin of presumption, just judgment. My presumptive experiences have similarly resulted with severe consequences. Without a word, I had no faith and thus no authority. My plans would be resisted, and disaster would result.

AUTHORITY

We often move into realms in which we have no authority to function. God has authority in the entire universe and beyond, so when He speaks, things change. We only have authority where we have been assigned and have been fruitful. Within our realm of authority, no matter how limited, we, like God, can create our own universe. God is sovereign over everything. What He says happens because His authority is absolute. He has created us in His image as men to function just like Him. Jesus was the exact representation of the Father and He challenged His disciples, saying, "...the works that I do shall he do also; and greater..." (John14:12). He raised the dead, gave sight to blind eyes, restored limbs, created food from next to nothing, produced money, and commanded obedience from the weather and the elements. He was being creative by simply speaking what He saw His Father doing. We, likewise, can do what we hear from Him, believing and declaring the will of the Father in our realm of authority.

Man was originally commanded to: "Be fruitful, and multiply, and replenish the earth, and subdue it: and have dominion over the fish...the [birds]...and over every living thing...upon the earth" (Gen. 1:28). The realm of the whole earth required more than one couple to subdue it. In our personal lives, we are absolute monarchs, but in corporate settings, we must come into agreement with other members of that community before we can enact God's will. It is like electing a government; there needs to be a majority in agreement to enact a decision. In the Kingdom, a majority is not required, just a core group, a remnant of believers, to enact God's legislation. The larger the realms (the more people involved), the more corporate the declaration must be for things to change.

Abraham did not have authority in Sodom, but Lot did because he lived there. Abraham could not stop the destruction on that city because he had no authority there. Lot needed the agreement of at least nine other people to be able to change a judgment, but he could not get that much agreement (see Gen. 18:32). Thus he had no power to stop the destruction. Abraham could intercede for Sodom, but Lot, and the corporate body of believers in Sodom, had to enact the deal that Abraham had negotiated. Unfortunately there was not sufficient faith in the community. Every function of the Kingdom follows the same faith principle: hear, believe, declare. We are designed to operate literally as God does, but we can't execute "vengeance and punishment" at our good pleasure. We can't bind "kings and nobles" as we feel like. We must hear what God is saying, believe it, come into agreement with it, and declare it in order to execute "judgment written; this honor have all His saints" (Ps. 149:7-9).

Just as we can create our own universe by speaking positively when we exercise faith, so also we create negative things when we declare unbelief. God said to Israel, "As ye have spoken in Mine ears, so will I do to you: your carcasses shall fall in this wilderness..." (Num. 14:28-29). What had the Israelites said that caused God to respond to them so harshly? They said, "If only we had died in this wilderness" (Num. 14:2 NKJV). I am sure that they didn't want to all be lined up and shot. It was just an expression of their unbelief, but they had the authority to create their own universe, and it happened just like they spoke.

We must be careful even how we jest or complain because "every idle [unprofitable] word that men shall speak, they shall give account [of] in the judgment" (Matt. 12:36). We always express what is in our hearts. We will exhibit "the same spirit of faith, according as it is written, I believed, and therefore have I spoken" (2 Cor. 4:13). Whether faith or fear, trust or disgust, it will come out and either bless our situation or curse it. That is why "the heart of the wise teaches his mouth, and adds learning to his lips" (Prov. 16:23 NKJV). We must learn to speak only faith because "whatsoever is not of faith is sin" (Rom. 14:23). God is training us to talk like Jesus, the "High Priest of our profession" (Heb. 3:1). He is training us to be proactive not reactive in our speech. This proactive stance makes us creative. We must take the initiative and "decree a thing, and it shall be established" (Job 22:28).

Our oldest adopted daughter, Vicky, had terrible eczema on her hands when she was young. Jeanne and I would pray for her and, as parents, declare her healing. One time the open, bleeding sores were completely healed right before our eyes, within half an hour. Other times nothing would happen. It was confusing having power that healed one minute and seemed to do nothing the next, but God was training us to think outside of our box. Grace allowed us to enact a creative miracle when Vicky was healed, but God was trying to teach us to discover the roots behind the fruit of the eczema that allowed it to come back. Sickness is one of the results of the Fall of Adam, and whether sickness is demonic or just empowered by the demonic is still debated.

Jesus used both approaches, rebuking and healing sicknesses. Vicky is part Inuit and came from a culture that had a history of animism (worshiping animal spirits). She was a fantastic artist, but her drawings were often grotesque and filled with violence that an eight-year-old girl would not normally picture. Jeanne started to notice a pattern; every time Vicky would be heavy into drawing these animal pictures in her schoolbooks, her eczema would get worse. We started to suspect demonic activity. One Saturday we went as a family to the provincial museum to view an Inuit art exhibit. There before our eyes were drawings of their gods that were identical to the ones Vicky had drawn.

We were very young, and the church we attended did not believe in this kind of demonic connections. The pastor was reluctant to approach the problem from that angle; after all, Vicky was so sweet; how could she entertain demons? He did agree one Sunday to pray for her healing. The pastor prayed for her in the morning service, and that night he took me aside and showed me his arms. They were all covered with eczema! The pastor said, "The devil spoke to me this morning and told me that if I prayed for her he was going to put the eczema on me. But it is a lie, he can't hold me." Sure enough, two days later the entire rash was gone.

We have to have enough wisdom and be humble enough to receive instruction from God. With the right weapons, we can be powerful. As for Vicky, as long as she refused to draw the demonically inspired pictures, her eczema stayed away. We have a part to play in our healing and must cooperate with God.

Twenty years ago, I had a personal revelation of this principle. I was at a very low time in my Christian walk and had little faith. My knee had been injured several years before, and I was in need of cartilage surgery. Every time I used the knee, it would swell up to the point that it appeared as if I had two kneecaps. Jeanne and I went to a camp meeting that spring. A former pastor of ours was preaching, and at the end of his sermon, he gave a call for healing. I had no intention of going forward. I was low in faith and too proud to admit that I needed any help. The healing ministry at the front took about 20 minutes. When it was over, the speaker said, "I feel like there is one more person whom God wants to touch. There is a problem with your knee, but you are too proud to come forward. If you respond, God says He will heal you."

There may as well have been a flashing light on my head. I knew I had to go up, but I was still expecting nothing. I wasn't disappointed; I got just what I expected, nothing.

Several months passed, and my spiritual condition was improving. I got a word from God that I was to go into the King of the Klondike competition. This was both a strongman and an endurance contest. I was not in great shape, so I started some conditioning training. I just put on some shorts and headed out the door. I had gone about 100 yards when my knee gave out. I remember trying to shake out my leg and manipulate my knee so that I could even walk. As I limped around in a circle for a minute wondering what to do, I meditated on the words God had spoken to me. I knew that God had said that I was healed, and I knew that He told me to go into this competition. Here I was in the middle of a gravel road hardly able to walk. I had a choice to make. Either the words were true or the symptoms were true. What was I going to believe?

I finally pulled up my courage and repented. I asked God to forgive me for being so proud and independent. I claimed my healing and declared, "On the basis of Your Word, I am going to train for this competition even if my leg falls off." I started to run, and I have never had trouble with my knee since. I had to cooperate with the word to create the healing that God had spoken months earlier.

I am learning that I don't just say what I have; I am learning how to have what I say. In the early 1980s, Jeanne and I were sent to England to explore the possibility of living there while I worked on a couple of construction projects. While we were looking at houses and apartments, we realized that the interest rates were over 20 percent! That was astronomical, even for then. The mortgage we had on our house in Alberta was due to be renewed in four years. We felt a warning from the Lord to get out of our mortgage, but we were not making the kind of money that would make that possible. God said, "Call it in."

Our prayers often seem to go unanswered because we are praying our own thoughts and desires. Real prayer is always birthed in the heart of God. We just need to hear and come into agreement. *To get a specific answer we need to pray a specific prayer.* God prompted us to ask for specific amounts of extra money that we could put on the mortgage for every anniversary date. Each year we claimed a particular sum; each year it would appear. Once we forgot when the payment was due and asked the bank what the date was. For some reason they told us it was July instead of June. We had no money in June but miraculously in July it appeared. When we went to pay, the bank would not accept the money and said we were too late. When they found out that it had been their error, they took the money. God works even when we can't. At the end of the four years, the entire mortgage had been retired. We were debt free and didn't have to renew when the rate jumped to over 20 percent here. We "have not, because [we] ask not" (James 4:2).

We are "joint-heirs with Christ" (Rom. 8:17). God puts us in the same category as Jesus, and we receive our inheritance with Him. That being the case, we must start to sound like Him and come into agreement with Him. To do that we must understand how God uses words and faith together. "Through faith we understand that the worlds were framed by the word of God" (Heb. 11:3). "He sent His word, and healed them" (Ps. 107:20). God uses words to create the things that are in His heart.

God also operates in faith. We are told to "have faith in God" (literally, the faith of God) (see Mark 11:22). The God-head is always in agreement when they speak, thus they are One. This oneness of heart and voice is faith. They agree and speak the same thing; that is faith. Our faith is exactly the same: we hear God, agree, and speak the same thing.

This connection between faith/power and words was demonstrated by the centurion when he said to Jesus, "Speak the word only, and my servant shall be healed. For I am a man under authority, having soldiers under me: and I say to this man, Go, and he [goes]; and to another, Come, and he [comes].... When Jesus heard it, He marvelled and said...I have not found so great faith, no, not in Israel" (Matt. 8:8-10). The centurion recognized true authority and the ability to exercise that authority with words. Jesus expressed that trusting in and operating in that relationship was faith. The power of the words comes from trusting the One in whom we have faith.

"Without faith it is impossible to please Him, for he who comes to God must believe that He is, and that He is a rewarder of those who diligently seek Him" (Heb. 11:6). We must believe that we will receive a reward for what we do in the Lord, or God is not pleased. I am not talking the "name it and claim it" or "blab it and grab it" type of faith but a relationship of love with the one we are agreeing with.

How would you feel if, on Christmas morning, your children got up and prepared to go over to the neighbors' house? If you asked them what they were doing and one replied, "Oh, I didn't think we were going to have any fun here today so I wanted to go next door," you would be devastated. I have a friend, Jozsi, who actually did that as a child. He related to me that the neighbor taught him how to build things by letting Jozsi do the job. Jozsi's own father just made him watch while he worked. The neighbor didn't care if Jozsi made mistakes. They developed a relationship, which Jozsi didn't have at home. It was a relationship built on love and acceptance.

On Christmas morning, after the family time around the tree, Jozsi would head next door and spend the day with his adopted family. I would have been devastated as a parent if my kids had done that. Parents want to bless their children and try to instill in them an expectation of good things. Parents aren't upset when their children expect presents, rather the opposite. It is the same with God. We haven't understood the heart of the Father if we don't recognize that He wants to bless us. "It is your Father's good pleasure to give you the Kingdom" (Luke 12:32). True faith, built on relationship, expects to receive good from God's hand. True relationships can relate heart to heart. We need to see God's heart, to come in agreement and act in faith.

Therefore, for faith to be activated, it must see from Heaven's perspective. We cannot do the work of God unless we see as God sees, and to see as He sees, we must think what He thinks. If we are in relationship, if we are friends, God will show us what He thinks and is about to do (see John 15:15). If we are not in relationship, then God says, "My thoughts are not your thoughts, neither are your ways My ways, [says] the Lord. For as the heavens are higher than the earth, so are My ways higher than your ways, and My thoughts than your thoughts" (Isa. 55:8-9).

Faith is not a formula. Faith is an expression of trust, of our friendship with God. Once we understand our relationship, then we can trust His word in the same way we trust Him. God says, "My word...it shall not return unto Me void, but it shall accomplish that which I please, and it shall prosper in the thing whereto I sent it" (Isa. 55:11). God's word has power resident in it to change situations, even in nature. Jesus spoke to the storm and even the winds and water obeyed Him (see Luke 8:25). Jesus intends us to function in like manner and do "greater works than these" (John 14:12). His words, spoken by us, also have the power to influence nature and the smaller storms in our lives.

Our son Shannon had pneumonia when he was a toddler, and it was bad enough that he needed to be hospitalized. Jeanne went to the hospital to be with him in the morning. She had been praying for Shannon and that morning felt that God had healed him; so she told the doctor that she was going to take him home. The doctor was furious, but Jeanne prevailed and took Shannon home. That Friday she took him back to the doctor's office as he had asked her to. The doctor brought in an associate to confer with, and Jeanne relayed that she had kept Shannon inside that week as a precaution. After examining Shannon, the doctor replied, "Why is this boy inside? He should be out playing." Jeanne had activated her faith and received a healing for our son as a result. Faith needs to be active. It needs to get out of the boat. However, you must have a word to act on or else you will be acting in presumption and that will not change anything.

God intends to have His word change things. Not just His word, but also ours mixed with His. Jeanne was at a prophetic school in Redding, California, when she got a bladder infection. It got so bad that she needed to leave class every hour to go to the washroom. Being from Canada, she wasn't sure that she had any medical coverage in the United States, so she didn't want to go to a doctor. She went to a pharmacy, but they couldn't give her anything to fight the infection without a prescription. So she prayed and claimed her healing. Immediately it started to clear up, and by the time she got home, she was completely better.

Miracles are always two-sided: the natural and the spiritual, God and man. This principle was illustrated in the story of Peter walking on the water. Peter had enough sense to understand the power of Jesus' word, so he asked, "Lord…bid me come" (Matt. 14:28), and Jesus replied, "Come" (Matt. 14:29). On the basis of that word, Peter got out of the boat and started to walk. Now, when you think about it, Peter didn't really do anything extraordinary. He did what he could have done had the boat been on dry ground. He walked. Peter had the ability to do that. He exercised his faith by trusting the word and getting out of the boat. The other 11 disciples, if they believed, could have come also, but they didn't. God's part in the miracle was holding up Peter so that he didn't sink. The water didn't hold him up. It didn't suddenly get hard, as was evidenced by the continuing action of the waves. Peter stood on the Word by faith. When faith was exchanged for sight, "when he saw the wind boisterous, he was afraid; and [began] to sink" (Matt. 14:30). The wind hadn't changed, but Peter's response to it had.

Hebrews explains what happened. "The word preached did not profit them [like Peter], not being mixed with faith" (Heb. 4:2). Peter's fear became mixed with the word, and that word could no longer support Peter, because it wasn't mixed with faith. Our battles occur because we are attempting to walk in two kingdoms. That is similar to having one foot on the dock and the other in the boat. That posture will eventually create a disaster. Paul said, "When I would do good, evil is present with me" (Rom. 7:21). We have unconverted areas within our souls that we have not yielded to the Lord. The blood cleanses our sins, but we must put our flesh on the cross to put it to death. Too many times we revive our flesh just before the deathblow is delivered. Sin and sickness were part of the atonement (see Isa. 53:4). The fact that sin and sickness still assail us doesn't mean the atonement didn't work; it means we have not been able to apply its virtue in every area of our lives.

That is what the battle is all about: our total redemption. The war is already won, but we must enforce it on our own battleground. Our part in the fight is to operate in light. We bring light the same way God brought light: we declare it. Jeanne always says, "I walk in divine health; I have divine healing." We must guard our own temple because there is an attack against us.

God created us as the stewards of this earth "to dress it and to keep it" (Gen. 2:15). That word *keep* means to hedge or guard or protect.[2] God knew that there was going to be an attack, and He warned Adam to guard against the attack. Adam was negligent in his duties, and satan slipped in, winning the first battle. Satan has no real authority. He occupies an office vacated of authority. I heard a story that John Dawson told comparing satan to a janitor who was cleaning an office tower at night. When everybody goes home, he goes into the corner office and sits at the manager's desk. He settles down into the soft leather, grabs a cigar from the box on the desk, and looks out over the city lights. He can imagine from there that he is the lord of all he surveys. In the morning, when the elevators start to hum and the staff returns, he must vacate the office or convince the staff that now he is in charge. If the staff is gullible, this charade could go on until the real manager shows up. That is what happened in the Garden to Adam and Eve, and that is what happens often in our lives.

Jeanne and I had bought our first house when we were in our early 20s. I was still fighting with lust in my life at that time, but I was trying to keep it hidden from my wife. I started having some lustful dreams and was fighting as much as my limited knowledge would allow me, but things were getting worse. Then Jeanne told me that she had a lustful dream. Now I knew I was in trouble; my wife, who is very prophetic, was tapping into my dreams. Through all this turmoil, I was still getting up early to spend time with God and read my Bible.

One night I had a pornographic dream, and as I was waking up, I saw a spirit, sort of a nebulous black cloud, go out the back door. I felt terrible and repented. Later that morning, I had one of the best revelations that God had ever given me. Now I was confused. *Why, if I was so evil and lustful that I was attracting demons, would God give me such revelation?*

I had not told Jeanne anything at that point. She was praying that morning after I went to work and felt the Lord prompting her to go up into the attic. She was afraid and didn't do anything at first, but God was insistent. We didn't have a ladder, so she shinnied up between the two walls in the hallway and opened the hatch. In the attic she found a box that the former owner had stashed away and forgotten. It was full of pornography. Jeanne prayed over all the stuff as she ripped it up and threw it out in the trash. She told me when I got home what had happened, so I confessed my problem to her. The interesting thing was that the dreams stopped immediately. Even though I had gone after the spirit myself, it would not leave until its stuff was removed. Spiritual stuff can be actual things in a physical location, as it was in this case, or things in us. Most of our battles would disappear if we were willing to deal with our stuff and stop hanging onto all the junk inside of us. God wants us to do a house cleaning so there is enough room for God to put some good stuff in our lives.

Jesus has since regained the position that Adam lost and re-stored all of our possessions. God gave us authority on the earth and commanded for man to have "dominion" over all the creatures on the earth (see Gen. 1:28). The Church is not walking in that experience of having dominion on the earth. We have adjusted our doctrine to fit what we see. We say, "Jesus must not have meant that," or "What He was really saying is this…." We must not do that anymore. Our job is still to guard the garden and have dominion over the earth.

If we actually believe that, and it still isn't working, then we will look for the reason why it isn't. If I know I have the right key to a door, but the door is not opening, I will keep trying until it does work. If I only hope I have the right key, and the door does not open, I will likely assume I have the wrong key and stop trying. We have the right keys! Jesus gave us the "keys of the kingdom" (Matt. 16:19). We have to align our thinking with what the Word says if we are to operate in faith. Faith is: hearing a word from God, believing that word, confessing or coming into agreement with the word, and then acting as if the word is true and has the necessary power.

This will often require us to change our whole way of thinking, our culture, or our current worldview. Abraham had to leave his country and relatives in order to enter into God's culture (see Gen. 12:1). A culture is a corporate way of thinking, talking, and acting. Jesus told the blind man not to go back into the city of Bethsaida lest he be talked out of his healing (see Mark 8:22-26) by the negative culture that existed there. Negative speech affects our faith (see 1 Cor. 15:33). We need to be people of faith and to stay around people who are going to speak faith. As vital as it is to believe, we must also speak out our faith like God, "who gives life to the dead and calls those things which do not exist as though they did" (Rom. 4:17 NKJV). That is Kingdom culture. God speaks things into existence, and so can we.

Jeanne found a house that she felt God had told her would be ours. It was a large house and was 50 percent more expensive than the one we were in. I prayed and got the same word as she received, but I didn't feel we should pay that much. We needed a strategy from God of how to proceed. He said, "Claim it. It's yours, but don't talk to anyone about it."

Our real estate agent was a Christian, so we told her that God had said we were not to negotiate with anybody about the property. We obeyed God and didn't deal with any real estate for three months. Nobody called us, and we made no inquiries. The real estate market was good at that time, but nobody bid on this house. One day, out of the blue, our friend called us and told us that the sellers were so upset with the way things were going that they were switching listing agents and dropping the price. She said that, if I wanted the house, we should get a hold of the new agent before the house got back on the market.

I promptly made a ridiculous offer (60 percent of the original asking price). The seller countered back only $5,000 higher, and the house was ours. The new house was 1,000 square feet bigger than the house we had been in but cost $8,000 less. That is creative financing; financing created by a word from God.

Part of faith is speaking into our situation the words God has spoken to us. Faith and unbelief are sitting at opposite ends of a teeter-totter. If faith is going up, unbelief goes down and vice versa. God once said to Jeanne and me that we were entering a harvest time. He said we would be reaping seeds that we had sown over the last 30 years. It was exciting. We paid down a $130,000 debt to $17,000 in just 13 months. In testifying to God's provision, I made the mistake of saying that God had said this was a harvest year. At the end of the year, the money dried up. I got what I said. Jeanne corrected me, and I repented for putting words in God's mouth that He had not said, and reclaimed the "harvest time" word. Over the next 18 months, we paid off the remaining $17,000 and another $150,000 on a house we bought. All this occurred after I retired and was only working about three months a year. It is not our righteousness that produced the harvest; it was properly declaring God's word.

We often think we have more faith if we feel we are walking in more personal righteousness or in doing things right. The reciprocal is actually true: we are imputed righteousness if we display more faith. "He [Abraham] staggered not at the promise of God through unbelief; but was strong in faith.... Therefore it was imputed to him for righteousness. It was not...for his sake alone...but for us also...it shall be imputed" (Rom. 4:20,22-24). Our righteousness depends on our faith, not our faith on our righteousness.

The great saints listed in Hebrews chapter 11, by faith, were translated, prepared an ark, received an inheritance, offered an only son, prophesied of things to come, chose to suffer affliction, subdued kingdoms, wrought righteousness, stopped lions, quenched fire, waxed valiant, received their dead back, while others were tortured, mocked, scourged, put in prison, stoned, and slain. All these received a good report through faith. Some succeeded; some failed. It was not the results that determined if they were in faith; it was believing God and walking with Him, no matter what.

I once heard Graham Cooke say that there are not good days and bad days but rather just days of grace. There are days of grace to enjoy and days of grace to endure. Both are useful in God's hand. Our son James was diagnosed with schizophrenia almost 15 years ago. In the beginning, he was in the hospital for months at a time, many times a year. Schizophrenia is a debilitating disease, and most people with this disease get worse, not better. As we searched for God's clarification on why this occurred, Jeanne read in the Bible that mental illness was part of a curse (see Deut. 28:28). She went back a chapter and found the root cause of the curse (see Deut. 27:15-26; Deut. 28:15,18). It was generational. Somewhere in the past, our families had entered into things that brought judgment down the family line. Jeanne interceded and asked for forgiveness back four generations and broke off the curse. Since then, James has not been back in the hospital and has gotten progressively better. *Our faithful God gives grace to endure and faith to overcome.*

As stated, our faith allows us to see things as God sees them. The soldier pinned down in a foxhole doesn't have the best perspective on how the war is going. If he is in communication with someone who can see, he can have grace to endure. We are in communion with God, so we can endure. He has promised to never leave us or forsake us (see Heb. 13:5). Through faith, then, we believe that "by the word of the Lord were the heavens made; and all the host of them by the breath of His mouth" (Ps. 33:6) and that "there is no power but of God: [and] the powers that be are ordained of God" (Rom. 13:1) and that Jesus has "all power...given unto [Him] in heaven and in earth" (Matt. 28:18). "What shall we then say to these things? If God be for us, who can be against us?" (Rom. 8:31). Faith trusts God, not our feelings or our situations.

Here is an analogy to help us understand what God means when He said He has all the power. Suppose we were in an office tower and God says He has *all* the air in this tower. If He has all the air, how much is left for us? None. If God is almighty, how much might does satan have? None. If God made everything, and everything serves His purpose, and He has all the power, then it follows that God is actually in control. Nothing happens that He doesn't see and isn't concerned about.

God is trying to move us into the place where we can trust Him no matter how contrary things may seem (see John 7:24). The truth is that there is always a problem between the promise and the provision. There is always a desert between Egypt and Canaan. The desert is a place that appears exactly opposite to the Promised Land. *Faith is not discouraged or disheartened by delays.* Faith believes and declares the provision, actually speaking it into being.

Jeanne was diagnosed with bowel cancer eight years ago. We sought a word from the Lord on what our posture should be. Did He want us to claim healing, deal with some root cause, or what? We actually heard nothing, so we kept going down the course that the doctors suggested, which was surgery.

When we cannot hear or see what God wants, when we are in fog, so to speak, then we should maintain the same course. When airline pilots go into a cloud, they are taught to maintain the original heading until new bearings can be seen. We need a clear word from God to change directions. So we went ahead with the surgery. The doctors removed a large tumor and 12 inches of the large intestine and 12 inches of the small intestine. Now she was facing chemo and radiation treatments.

At this point, Jeanne and I had a large negative reaction in the spirit. Neither one of us wanted her to go through this regimen, but we still had no word. Many people had been praying for her, and God used the Body to bring what we could not get for ourselves. Two different members of the church got different visions; but both said the same thing: the cancer was contained. In other words, the cancer had not spread beyond the intestinal wall.

The surgeon had taken out 37 lymph nodes from the abdomen because, in his opinion, they were all cancerous and he didn't want to perform a second operation. These nodes were sent off to the cancer clinic for biopsies. Armed with our own sense of what the Spirit wanted and the confirmation of the two words of containment, Jeanne challenged the surgeon on his diagnosis. She asked him what would happen if the tests came back normal. He responded that he had been doing this for 20 years and knew a cancerous lymph node when he saw one and would not entertain her question. This was the top cancer surgeon in the area, and other than the Spirit speaking the opposite, I had no reason to doubt his diagnosis.

Two weeks later we went to the cancer clinic to get set up for the radiation therapy. The head doctor came into the examining room and looked at Jeanne. I mean *looked*. He didn't examine her; he just stared at her for a good 20 seconds. Jeanne had armed herself in prayer to resist a spirit of fear that was so heavy in the building. There was joy and faith all over her. You could tell he was looking at something around her or in her countenance that he could not explain. Finally he spoke to her.

He said, "Normally in these kinds of operations, we take out 5 or 6 lymph nodes just to check their condition. Even if these nodes are clean, we would still run you through radiation and chemo just to be sure we get everything. Your lymph nodes looked so bad that the surgeon removed them all. Because he took out so many, and they all came back clean, you don't need any radiation or chemotherapy. See you in six months for a checkup."

That was eight years ago. Faith has the ability to change the "facts" and replace them with the truth. The facts suggested the lymph nodes were cancerous; the truth was that Jesus had healed Jeanne. We always have to go through the valley of testing after we get the promise, but God goes with us.

I have often heard Joyce Meyer say that God wants to bring us from the land of just enough (desert) to the land of more than enough (Promised Land). To accomplish this, God instituted a covenant. In this covenant, He promises on His part to do certain things and then promises to help you do your part: "'This is My covenant with them,' saith the Lord; 'My Spirit that is upon thee, and My words which I have put in thy mouth...'" (Isa. 59:21). Our power and authority comes not only from the Spirit in us but through our declarations. However, our tongues don't always declare what God is saying. We say a lot of what we are feeling. This ambiguous speaking is a good indication of how much mixture is in us.

The children of Israel were not the only people to leave Egypt in the Exodus. A mixed multitude of many peoples left with them. It was this mixture that caused them to complain. "The mixt multitude that was among them fell a lusting: and the children of Israel also wept" (Num. 11:4). They started to look back to the "good old days." "We remember the fish, which we did eat in Egypt freely [that was probably a lie]; the cucumbers...melons...leeks...onions and the garlick" (Num. 11:5). God had promised freedom and the land of milk and honey. They were complaining while passing through the desert. This complaining was a sign of their lack of faith in the word God spoke. Because God wanted to work through them, this complaining short-circuited the power that was to be theirs and cut them off from the promise. It is the mixture of flesh in us that produces our complaints.

So how do we defeat the flesh in us? We defeat the fleshly thoughts with words, not other thoughts. Jesus did this when satan came to tempt Him. He "answered and said, 'It is written'" (Matt. 4:4). God expects us to speak the same way. We are told to let the high praises of God be in our mouths to execute vengeance and punishments, to bind, to execute upon them the judgment written because "...this honour have all His saints..." (see Ps. 149:6-9). Negative thoughts will always assail us; we are in a war. It is a war of words. The weapons we use to fight these negative thoughts are positive, spiritual words, words like Jesus used. "The weapons of our warfare are...mighty...bringing into captivity every thought to the obedience of Christ" (2 Cor. 10:4-5). We need to work together with Jesus to maintain right thoughts.

From the beginning, God and Adam worked together in exercising creative authority on the earth. God created the animals and brought them to Adam "to see what he would call them: and whatsoever Adam called every living creature, that was [its] name" (Gen. 2:19). The same principle acts now; God has the creative power, and we have the authority to call it what it is. So again, it is not so much saying what we have, but having what we say. Our speaking is the response of faith, declaring into those areas that we have been given authority over.

I have a friend, Ron, who had arthritis in his feet so bad that he was having a hard time walking. I shared with him about the healing I received for my knee. He didn't have much faith to believe that God would do the same for him. After much encouragement, he prayed and received his healing. When I asked him if he was healed, he gave the most common answer, "I think so." We went through the teaching again about him participating in his own healing by voicing a positive (not a maybe) confession. This time he said, "I am healed." I challenged him, "If you are healed then we should go for a run." He agreed and off we went for a mile jog. His faith and corresponding action has allowed him to keep his healing for the last 25 years.

We have authority to call things what they are because God gave that authority to Adam, and then, after we lost it, God purchased it back for us through Jesus. Jesus said that He has the keys to hell and death (see Rev. 1:18). Those keys open our doors to freedom.

No more can satan intimidate us because he cannot dictate our death. This power is in the hands of our loving God. We now have the power of an endless life. Jesus said that "whoever believes in Him should not perish but have eternal life" (John 3:15 NKJV). Think about that! If we are walking in the will of God, nothing can in any way hurt us. Knowing this creates boldness, which is the sign of real authority. This faith in our authority causes us to act and talk like we have authority. People and situations respond to legitimate authority by simply coming under it.

The chief priests and Pharisees sent officers to arrest Jesus. When the officers came under the authority of Jesus' words, they couldn't obey the priests' lesser authority. They came back to the priests empty-handed. The chief priest asked, "'Why have you not brought Him?' The officers answered, 'No man ever spoke like this man'" (John 7:45-46 NKJV). Jesus knew who He was, and when He spoke, others responded to His authority. If we don't know who we are, then we will walk in unbelief and have no power.

UNBELIEF

The opposite of faith is unbelief. Unbelief manifests itself in disobedience and an inability to trust in God. Inability to operate in faith brings a completely different outcome than operating in faith. By faith, Israel passed through the Red Sea on dry land, but when the Egyptians attempted the same thing, they drowned (see Heb. 11:29). The Egyptians tried to do the same things as Israel, but without faith, and they perished.

Today much of the new age movement has picked up on the principles, but they don't walk in a relationship with God and, therefore, don't operate in faith. The Church should not be afraid of the new age philosophies. We need to recognize them for what they are: counterfeits. Good counterfeits are almost indistinguishable from the real thing. If there is a counterfeit, then there is a real. We as a Church have abandoned many of the realms of the supernatural because they are used by the new age. We should repent and recover these areas of truth.

The new age movement saw what God was doing and occupied those areas while the Church was stagnating in tradition. They may see through a distorted lens, but they see. We, the Church, should see clearly, but we won't look and have assigned much of the spiritual areas to the occult. That is why they seem to have more power than the church—although they don't.

There are three main roots to unbelief or rejection of truth:

1. Bad Experiences

In the time just before the Church arose, there had been several insurrections in Israel. Charismatic leaders, who had led away many, led these uprisings. The temple leadership was unwilling, because of their bad experiences, to even hope that this Nazarite sect was anything but trouble. So when Peter and John came before them, the leaders wanted to kill them (see Acts 5:33).

2. Tradition

Our mindset (the set pattern of our thoughts) precludes receiving truth in any form other than those that fit our expectation or traditions. Jesus tried to explain to Peter about His crucifixion. Peter's traditional theology, about a conquering Messiah, did not allow him to comprehend a suffering Messiah—even though it was in the Scriptures. He went so far as to tell Jesus (whom he knew was the Messiah) that He was wrong. "Peter took Him [Jesus], and began to rebuke Him" (Mark 8:32). It is interesting that, even though the chief priests and scribes knew that the Messiah was to be born in Bethlehem (see Matt. 2:4-5), none of them went with the wise men to find Jesus. Their traditions couldn't accommodate a baby Messiah, even though every other king had to be a baby at some time. *Our traditions and theology often blind us from a proper examination of the truth and all of its implications.*

3. Fear

Peter was seemingly fearless. All by himself, he stood up to fight the mob in the garden, the night Jesus was betrayed. But fear, which actually has its roots or hooks in doubt (about God's love and care, about our place, about what the world says), is a spirit. It chooses when it will attack and in what manner. If there is an unhealed area that allows doubt to exist, this becomes the spot where that spirit can put in a hook and manifest itself. Peter was brave enough to get out of the boat and walk on water (see Matt. 14:28-31). However, fear arose when he saw the wind was so strong. Jesus identified the root: "You of little faith, why did you doubt?" (Matt. 14:31 NKJV). In the boat Peter had a word to "Come" (Matt. 14:29). That word alone, when added to his faith, was able to allow him to defy the laws of nature and walk on the water. When he doubted, he nullified his faith and "the word...did not profit them, not being mixed with faith" (Heb. 4:2). The result? He sank.

I learned a good acronym for fear:

False
Evidence
Appearing
Real

The false evidence, for Peter, was the wind and the waves, which logic declared could not support his weight. The reality was, the Creator of the universe had told Peter that he could do the same thing his Master was doing. Our decision about which voice we obey dictates what we are allowed to do. Each of us has to face this conflict.

For years I had gout in both my big toes. It was so bad that I could not climb a ladder without a lot of pain. I knew how to get healed and went after it with vigor. I prayed and prayed. I prayed for ten years until I realized that I was still listening to the pain. I was trying to dictate to God what my healing was supposed to look like. So I stopped praying (which actually was more like whining and complaining) and just claimed health. Two years later, the pain was still there, and the toes still wouldn't bend, but I was not changing my stance.

Then one night, just before Christmas, I woke up at 2 A.M. I didn't know why I was awake. There had been no noise, yet something caused me to come out of a deep sleep. Then I realized that my big toes could wiggle, and they didn't hurt. My healing had manifested 12 years after I started praying, and my toes are perfect today. God is faithful, but some seeds take a longer time maturing. Most often it is us that takes the long time maturing.

That is why God told Moses what Pharaoh's reaction to his request for Israel's freedom was going to be and why He would allow the resistance. Moses was afraid because he didn't know who he was. He had tried 40 years before to save Israel supposing that "his brethren would have understood…that God by his hand would deliver them: but they understood not" (Acts 7:25). Now he was being sent back with the same mission to the same people. His lack of faith arose from his wounding concerning the first attempt, when he was rejected. God armed him with signs and wonders, but also with the words: "I will harden Pharaoh's heart…that I may lay My hand upon Egypt, and bring forth Mine armies, and My people the children of Israel, out of the land of Egypt by great judgments" (Exod. 7:3-4). These words were designed to help Moses through the tough times that were coming.

God also prepared Israel, through progressive difficulties after they left Egypt, to be able to conquer the land of Canaan. This was to build their faith, for God knew their mindset. He didn't take them the short way to the Promised Land "lest perhaps the people change their minds when they see war, and return to Egypt" (Exod. 13:17 NKJV). Our faith is built incrementally to be able to withstand a stronger and stronger enemy. Passing all the tests in grade 1 simply qualifies us to take the tests in grade 2. It has been said, "new level, new devil." God's will is to "harden you to difficulties" (Isa. 41:10 AMP).

I have heard people say, "Don't pray for patience because then situations that try your patience will come." They have no concept of the purpose for our existence. We were created in the presence of an enemy; the snake was in the Garden. We are designed in God's image: "The Lord is a man of war" (Exod. 15:3), and we are to be a "battle axe and weapons of war…[to] break in pieces the nations" (Jer. 51:20). We are not to be fearful and unbelieving. We need a real enemy to get a real victory. The greater the conflict, the greater the victory. That is why God told Moses, "I indeed will harden the…Egyptians, and they shall follow…so I will gain honor" (Exod. 14:17). The Israelites panicked when they saw Pharaoh pursuing them. They didn't realize that God was building a reputation for Israel that in the future would put fear into their enemies' hearts. The first person Israel encountered in Canaan said, "The terror of you has fallen on us…we have heard how the Lord dried up the water of the Red Sea for you" (Josh. 2:9-10 NKJV). We need to trust God more and realize that the problems we encounter now are designed to hold us in good stead later.

We want to honor God, and our being in a good fight beside Him is one of the best ways to do that. Of course, only a fight you win is a good fight! So God will incrementally get us ready for war. It all starts with our thoughts, which will dictate our actions. Consistency in actions is defined as habits. Our habits will influence our disposition to do what is right. Our disposition rightly aligns our will. Strength in our will becomes our character. Proper character makes us look like Jesus because we are "conformed to the image of His Son [Jesus]" (Rom. 8:29). If we look and act like Him, we will not be afraid to lay down our lives as He did. And if we "suffer, we shall also reign with Him" (2 Tim. 2:12). That is true authority, but you must mix the seed of the word with faith in order to reap.

Our justification is by faith (see Rom. 5:1). Faith is the door into grace (see Eph. 2:8) that allows God to walk with us and change us. He is a holy God, and without grace (undeserved favor) we would receive judgment. God uses situations to change us. Most of our prayers are for our situations to change, but God wants *us* to change. The situations are nothing. Situations are designed to be the canvases upon which we inscribe the Kingdom of God. We need to change the way we view the situations God puts us in so they will profit us, not defeat us.

Once we are converted (changed in our thinking), then we can glory in "tribulations... [which works] patience; and patience, experience; and experience, hope" (Rom. 5:3-4). Hope allows us to believe for the character and love necessary to move to the next level of authority. Jesus speaks His authority: "Out of His mouth goes a sharp sword [word], that with it He [will] strike the nations" (Rev. 19:15 NKJV). We need to have faith in what the Word says if we are to operate in that kind of authority. We can speak like that if we recognize that we are ambassadors of God. When war is declared, the ambassador delivers the declaration. When a treaty is enacted, the ambassador's signature seals the agreement. He is the official voice of the country he represents. We are not poor little Christians trapped in this evil world praying desperately for deliverance. We are Heaven's emissaries, and we have immunity in the country we reside in. In fact, the embassy is considered foreign soil, and those who escape into its sanctuary are safe. The ambassador may understand the language of the country he lives in, but his native tongue is (usually) different. We are ambassadors (see 2 Cor. 5:20). We are not only free to keep the customs of our King, who we represent, but we are expected to maintain those customs.

The ambassador of a country that has conquered the other nation is in an even stronger position of enforcing terms of the victory. He can dictate to the leaders of that country the wishes of the victor. He can imprison them if he desires. So we can "bind their kings with chains, and their nobles with fetters of iron; to execute upon them judgment written: this honor have all His saints" (Ps. 149:8-9). But like an ambassador, we have no opinions of our own. We simply represent Him who sent us. Don't let any "doctrine of demons" cause you to think that hard times and great persecution do not await the Church, even in North America. We must speak our victory, not because the battle is over, but because it is just beginning. Let the "redeemed of the Lord say so, whom He has redeemed from the hand of the enemy" (Ps. 107:2 NKJV).

God is not subject to time and space. The victory can be delivered because it has already been accomplished. Our faith is what brings a manifestation of that victory into our realm of authority (the earth). "Have faith [the firm conviction that comes from hearing] in God" (Mark 11:22). Faith is a language that emanates from Heaven. Our ability to hear and to declare what we hear activates those words. Faith is futuristic. It can see the past, but it is designed to frame the future, and it allows us to enjoy the present.

Jesus is our example in everything, and we look to "Jesus the author and finisher of our faith; who for the joy that was set before Him endured the cross" (Heb. 12:2). We must entrust our souls to God. He will give us a joy for today, if we can, with faith, see the promise as a reality. Each of us has a cross that we must endure. God is fashioning our lives, and everything we go through is part of the development of our character. So, "suck it up, buttercup." God is the God of our situations. We can trust Him. He calls on us to build ourselves up in our faith, praying in the Holy Ghost (praying in tongues), and to keep ourselves in the love of God, looking for the mercy of our Lord Jesus Christ unto eternal life (see Jude 20-21).

That's our job:

> Build up our own spirits.
> Keep ourselves in God's love.
> Look for (expect) God's mercy.

Much of the Church has been in bondage and prison houses, under a curse, because we trusted in things other than God (see Isa. 42:18-25). But God, upon whom our faith is fixed, is about to do a new thing (see Isa. 42:9). Our part is to hear what He is saying and to not despise the day of small beginnings (see Zech. 4:10); rather, we must recognize them as the seeds. We must also speak words to water these seeds of restoration (see Isa. 42:22).

God has shown us what is coming. We must give Him His words back in agreement so that He can work on our behalf. God desires us to work with Him. He is willing, prophetically, to show us things. "Ask Me of things to come concerning My sons [and He wants to speak and activate these prophetic pictures]; and concerning the work of My hands, you command Me" (Isa. 45:11 NKJV).

Some translators couldn't fathom that God actually wants us to give Him orders about the earth; and in a way, they are right. What God wants to do is to change us so completely that our will is completely aligned with His. In that state, He can then do our will. The original Hebrew, *tsavah*, is not asking a question. The Hebrew root of the word *command* means to charge, or send a messenger, and to put in order.[3] That is how God wants us to act after we know His will.

For example, we do this when we go into a restaurant. The waitress and the cook are prepared to serve you. You are not in charge of the establishment; they are; but they are there to serve you. They cannot give you anything that they have prepared until you do one thing: give your order. God has many good things prepared for them that love Him. Just speak His words and watch what God will do. God is telling us to hear His word, believe it, and speak it back to Him as a declaration so that He can move on our behalf. That is faith, and it is one of the characteristics that God loves.

ENDNOTES

1. Spiros Zodhiates, *The Complete Word Study New Testament* (Chattanooga, TN: AMG Publishers, 1991), #3358/2583.

2. Zodhiates, *The Complete Word Study Old Testament* (Chattanooga, TN: AMG Publishers, 1992), #8104.

3. Zodhiates, *The Complete Word Study Old Testament*, #6680.

Chapter 3

An Anchor in the Storm—Hope

HOPE WILL SUSTAIN US

God spoke to me once that there are three things that will remain forever: faith, hope, and love (see 1 Cor. 13:13). He said that the world has hope as a future event, wishing for the best, and it has faith based on what happened in the past. God said to me, "That is the wrong order." The world uses the word *hope* in the context of wishful thinking or doubtful expectations about what will occur. It uses *faith*, rooted in the past, for what has been. An example might be, "I have faith in the banks because they have never lost my money," or "I have faith in the stability of the government because there have been no riots lately."

99

Neither of these concepts can produce any power however. The Christian concept is completely different—or should be.

God said that the actual function of faith should be futuristic, and hope should be based on the past, on what Jesus already accomplished on the cross. This hope then becomes "an anchor of the soul, both sure and steadfast" (Heb. 6:19 NKJV). In this configuration, both faith and hope are now creative and have substance, the "evidence of things not seen" (Heb. 11:1). Even though hope deals with something we are looking for, it has its expectation based on something solid and already accomplished: Jesus' death and resurrection.

"For him who is joined to all the living there is hope, for a living dog is better than a dead lion" (Eccles. 9:4 NKJV). As long as I draw breath I can hope. It's not over until it's over; and even when it's over, it's not over if hope is alive. We see this in Abraham's life as he was sent by God to Mount Moriah to offer Isaac as a sacrifice. When Isaac questioned his father about the lamb for the sacrifice, Abraham prophetically spoke that God would "provide Himself a lamb" (Gen. 22:8). God responded to Abraham's faith by providing "a ram caught in a thicket" (Gen. 22:13).

So Abraham called the place *Jehovah-Jireh* (the Lord will see and provide). But Abraham himself had already in his heart sacrificed Isaac. He had thought that God wanted to kill his son, not realizing that it was his own self-death that God wanted to accomplish.

Abraham's main struggle in his early faith life was to produce a child (seed) who would be his heir. God's original promise to Abraham, when he was 75 years old, was that, if he would go where God would send him, then He would make him a great nation. Abraham's battle to produce that seed (out of which Christ would arise) dominated every aspect of his life. He tried to convince God to accept his servant Eliezer as his heir because he was born in his house (see Gen. 15:2-3). Then he tried to produce a son through Sarah's maid. He again tried to convince God to accept Ishmael (see Gen. 17:18), but God had other plans. Abraham had heard the promise and believed that God would make him a great nation, but the understanding of the fulfillment came to him progressively.

Abraham responded as we do to God's promises by trying to see how it will work.

"Maybe Eliezer?"

"No! Your seed."

"Maybe Ishmael?"

"No! Your seed and Sarah's seed."

"Isaac?"

"Yes! Now sacrifice him!"

Abraham had been on this journey for 40 years to produce what God wanted, and now after Isaac was born, Abraham again had to let the promise die. He had grown in trust so much (by this time) that he never hesitated when called to sacrifice Isaac, but immediately responded. However, he thought he had figured out in his own mind what was going to happen.

God had done the impossible in allowing Sarah and Abraham to have a son, and now Abraham was looking to see God do the miraculous. He had reasoned that "God was able to [and going to] raise him up, even from the dead" (Heb. 11:19). Thus, in his own mind, Isaac was dead and he would receive him back from there (the place of the dead) when he took him off the altar.

Abraham's hope allowed him to believe God and produce a nation. Abraham "against hope believed in hope, that he might become the father of many nations" (Rom. 4:18). His *faith*, in carrying out his part of the agreement with God, was accounted as righteousness; but his *hope* produced his seed. As quoted earlier, the Book of Hebrews confirms that faith and hope are intertwined: "Faith is the substance of things hoped for, the evidence of things not seen" (Heb. 11:1). Hope then is not seen. "For we are saved by hope...for what a man seeth, why doth he yet hope for?" (Rom. 8:24). Yet the "worlds were framed by the word of God, so that the things which are seen were not made of things which are visible" (Heb. 11:3 NKJV).

What is being said here? The hope that God gives us does not have a visible manifestation at the time God speaks. Our friends, Clint and Karen, learned how to draw on the power that hope manifests for their own child. They had been trying to have a baby for eight years when Clint was diagnosed with testicular cancer. He needed an operation and radiation to eradicate the cancer. Either course of action would have been sufficient to make having a baby, already an untenable hope, impossible. Two years later, Clint's cancer reappeared. This time it showed up as two golf-ball-sized lumps in the lymph nodes in his neck. The doctor shifted the treatment to a regimen of chemotherapy, which killed the cancer, but it also killed their last hopes about their ability to have children. Now they could see no hope at all.

Yet there is another type of seeing, on a different plane. It is this seeing, of the promise in the spirit, that gives us hope. A prophet and his wife came to our church's conference one year after Clint's chemo. The prophet's wife called Clint and Karen forward for prayer. She asked Clint, "Do you want a child?" He had to draw down deep into his character to see if there was enough faith there to even hope anymore. Finally he responded, "Yes." She prayed that God would produce a miracle and give them a child and then added, "Mark this day. This child will be a sign to the church of the ability of God to perform His word and keep His promises."

One year later, Farrah was born: a healthy, 10-pound, 14-ounce baby girl.[1] Clint had to exercise faith and act like Abraham, "who against hope believed in hope, that he might become [a] father" (Rom. 4:18). Faith is the vehicle that allows what is seen in the spirit to manifest in our sight. Abraham's declaration that God would provide a lamb allowed him to see that ram in the thicket "behind" him: "Abraham lifted up his eyes, and looked, and behold behind him a ram" (Gen. 22:13). Where was the ram before? Why could he see it now?

The answer lies in a similar situation, which occurs just before this story, with Hagar, Abraham's concubine. On God's orders, Hagar and Ishmael, her son, had been sent away from

Abraham and Isaac, but they had run out of water and were dying of thirst. She started to cry, and an angel answered out of Heaven and spoke a word of hope to her saying, "Do not fear, for God has heard…. Arise…for I will make a great nation of him" (Gen. 21:17-18 NASB). In the midst of her trouble, God arrived and changed everything. Then "God opened her eyes, and she saw a well of water. And she went…and gave the lad a drink" (Gen. 21:19 NKJV).

What just happened? We read these accounts but often don't recognize what is being said. There they were, dying of thirst, desperate for water, but she couldn't see the well? Or was the well in another dimension: on the other side of the veil?

This expression, "God opened her eyes," appears in another place in the Bible that clarifies what is meant. The king of Aram had sent an army to capture Elisha the prophet. When his servant saw the army, he panicked; but Elisha was not concerned because he could see what the servant couldn't. After he tried to give the servant hope, Elisha asked God to "'open his eyes that he may see.' …And he saw…the mountain was full of horses and chariots of fire all around Elisha" (2 Kings 6:17 NKJV).

The "opening" of the servant's eyes allowed him to see into the spiritual realm and the vast angelic host that was there with them. The opening of Hagar's eyes allowed her not only to see, but also to go through the veil (that covers that realm) and bring sustenance back. There is a realm where all our supply is reserved for us. Jesus went into that realm to feed the 4,000 and the 5,000. On earth, He had limited resources, but in Heaven

He had abundance. Jesus was no poorer because He fed the multitudes, and He would have been no richer if He had not fed them. His supply did not depend on the money He had in the treasury. Jesus even set up a thief (Judas) as His treasurer because that was not the source of His supply; God was. We don't need wealth; we need abundance just like Jesus.

THE VEIL

Jesus has made a way for us to enter through the veil so that we may have "strong consolation, [we] who have fled for refuge to lay hold of the hope set before us. This hope we have as an anchor of the soul, both sure and steadfast, and *which enters...behind the veil...*where the forerunner [Jesus] has entered for us" (Heb. 6:18-20 NKJV). Jesus opened the way through the veil for us, on the cross, for when He yielded up His spirit, the veil of the temple was rent in two from top to bottom (see Matt. 27:50-51). Now, it was not just a priest with a sacrifice of blood who was allowed to enter; now *we* could also enter into the holiest place "by the blood of Jesus, by a new and living way...through the veil, that is to say, His flesh" (Heb. 10:19-20).

The Book of Acts declares that this situation is what God wants to prevail at the end of the age. God stated that He would rebuild the tabernacle of David in the last days. The significant difference between the tabernacle of David and the tent of meeting or the temple was that there was no veil in David's tabernacle, no separation between God and man. That difference allowed the people to actually *see* into spiritual dimensions.

"They have seen Thy goings, O God; even the goings of my God, my King, in the sanctuary" (Ps. 68:24).

What is the tool or attitude required to access this gate into Heaven? Hope! Hope enters within the veil (see Heb. 6:19). This veil can be crossed both ways. Jeanne and I had a spiritual experience during a time of real financial crisis. I had made an investment without hearing from God, and it had turned out badly, real badly. We were going to lose over $100,000. Jeanne had never agreed with this investment but had prayed and felt she should submit to my decision, after voicing her opinion. She then invoked what she called the Abraham/Sarah covenant. Sarah believed that God would protect her from suffering from Abraham's mistakes. "Sarah obeyed Abraham, calling him lord, and you [are] her children if you do what is right without...fear" (1 Pet. 3:6 NASB). Jeanne claimed this promise and could then have hope no matter what the situation of the investment.

We went to seek God (better late than never) in the living room. As we were praying, Jeanne saw Abraham in an open vision. He walked into the living room and spoke to her. He said, "Tell your husband that God is a redeemer, and He will redeem everything that has been stolen from you." She told me what she had seen and heard. I started to muse on what had just happened. I remembered what Abraham had done, putting Sarah into a harem for the second time. I felt like Abraham said, "Everything God had promised me, I threw away not once but twice. God redeemed her to me, and He will do the same for you."

I started to cry as I sensed how hopeless Abraham must have felt at that time, but I had hope because of the word the vision of Abraham had spoken. I now knew that God wanted to show His power and mercy to us. A short time later, God gave me a word. He said, "This is a harvest time. The seeds you have sown over the past 30 years are about to come to fruit." Over the next couple of years, God brought in more than double the amount that I had lost. The original investment never came back, but God was faithful to His word and restored what was stolen. That is the power of hope—hope that was based on what the Father had done for others. I could have faith that He would do the same for me because He loves me.

This hope then allows us to see the unseen, to see the promises, to see the Lord. Our walk as Christians is not about *doing* something but about *being* something. We are to "be like Him, because we will see Him just as He is" (1 John 3:2 NASB). Part of being like Him is to have the ability to see Him. To be able to see Him, we must be able to penetrate the veil. To go through the veil, we must have hope. "And everyone who has this hope fixed on Him purifies himself" (1 John 3:3 NASB). This purity allows us to see Him. "Blessed are the pure in heart: for they shall see God" (Matt. 5:8). So then purity allows us to see, hope allows us to see, and seeing gives us hope and causes us to purify ourselves, which gives us ability to see more, and on it goes. This is the calling of the Church as well as individuals.

The first mention of the Church (the house of God) in the Old Testament bears a striking resemblance to Jesus' New Testament description of Himself operating under an open Heaven.

"And he [Jacob] dreamed, and behold a ladder...reached to heaven...*angels of God ascending and descending*" (Gen. 28:12). "This is...the house of God...the gate of heaven" (Gen. 28:17). Jesus said, "You shall see heaven open [a gate], and the *angels of God ascending and descending* upon the Son of Man" (John 1:51 NKJV).

In both descriptions, we see that the veil, which separates Heaven from earth, is removed, allowing angelic activity to operate under that open Heaven. Both aspects of the Church as the Body of Christ and the dwelling place of God indicate that it is to be a gate or a place of opening. The veil or the covering was instituted by God and is held in place by the one originally anointed to do that: satan or lucifer. When the Bible describes satan, it says, "You were the anointed cherub who covers; I [God] established you" (Ezek. 28:14 NKJV). If God set up the covering or the veil, then there is a redemptive purpose for its existence at this present time.

God promises to destroy this covering from over the nations that keeps them from seeing Him. "He will destroy...the surface of the covering cast over all people, and the veil...spread over all nations" (Isa. 25:7). Corporately this happens when a critical mass of believers in a specific geographic area come under an anointing that has a pure motive to reveal Jesus. This has happened during the major revivals over the last few centuries and lately in Toronto, Canada, and Brownsville, Florida.

I have witnessed an open portal in my own city of Edmonton over the last five years. A team of prophetic evangelists and intercessors has come under the apostolic covering of Every

Home for Jesus Ministries. This is a ministry headed up by Rita and Lorne Silverstein that reaches into the marketplace with the cooperation of over 30 diverse churches. One outreach, The Angels Booth, uses trade show settings as the vehicle for evangelism. Most evangelism is still operating from the premise that the target audience has a Christian tradition somewhere in their past. In today's multicultural and post-Christian society, that most often is not the case. With no knowledge or appreciation of the Bible, our quoting it, as the source of truth, just turns people away. We need to meet them where they are: with little or no knowledge of Jesus or the Father.

We used the vehicle of dream interpretation and spiritual readings (prophetic encouragement) to pique their attention. Once they indicated an interest in spiritual things, they could be introduced to Jesus as the way through the veil to the Father. The booth had awesome success. People who may have won only a handful of souls to the Lord over their lifetime were winning up to 40 and 50 people in one five-hour shift at the booth. With up to 85 workers, salvations totaled over 2,400 in just ten days. This phenomenon has been going on for years. The salvations cut across all faiths and cultures, yet without that particular anointing that opened Heaven, few of the team has ever been able to duplicate, in a year, what was accomplished there in an hour. The anointing over the booth removed the veil over that physical area.

Similarly in individual lives, that "vail is upon their heart...when it [their heart] shall turn to the Lord, the vail shall be taken away" (2 Cor. 3:15-16). So the veil is there because a man's heart is hardened and he does not want the light to shine on his evil deeds. The desire to avoid light is our first clue that something is wrong. "The god of this world [has] blinded the minds of them which believe not, lest the light...of Christ...should shine unto them" (2 Cor. 4:4). Satan can't do whatever he wants. God is in control, but He still uses satan to fulfill His purposes.

Jesus' disciples asked Him, "Why do You speak to them in parables?" And Jesus answered, "I speak to them in parables, because seeing they do not see, and hearing they do not hear.... 'For the hearts of this people have grown dull. Their ears are hard of hearing, and their eyes they have closed, lest they should see...and hear...lest they should understand with their hearts and turn, so that I should heal them'" (Matt. 13:10,13,15 NKJV).

I thought that was the whole intention of Jesus' coming: getting people to understand, to convert, and to be healed. Now this passage would sound more like He is cooperating with satan rather than trying to deliver people from him, except we know that everything God does has a loving, redemptive purpose. It is God's mercy that blinds them when their hearts are hard and there is no intent to obey. Paul wrote that "...the election hath obtained it [the promise], and the rest were blinded" (Rom 11:7) and that "...blindness in part is happened to Israel.... For God hath concluded them all in unbelief, that He might have mercy upon all" (Rom. 11:25,32). In order to not have to bring them under judgment, because of their knowing disobedience, God blinds them to the truth and leaves them ignorant in sin so that He can bring them to a place where He can show mercy. He did this for Israel; He does it for us also because "mercy triumphs [rejoices] over judgment" (James 2:13 NKJV). This is why people don't see: there is no intent to obey. We can't see without revelation, anyway, until God in His mercy changes this hardness by bringing trouble into our lives to discipline us individually and corporately. The state of our hearts will determine our ability to see and be healed and delivered. That principle is reiterated by Paul when he says concerning Israel, "Their minds were blinded...[and a] ...vail is upon their heart. Nevertheless when it [the heart] shall turn to the Lord, the vail shall be taken away" (2 Cor. 3:14-16).

THE DISCIPLINE

This is the purpose of trouble. God allows us to hit the bottom so that we will have "no confidence in the flesh" (Phil. 3:3). As long as we attempt to work out our righteousness by self-effort and the exercising of our will, we will fail. That is a work of the flesh, and even though it appears good, it will eventually put us at cross purposes to God's will. Israel is our example, who "pursuing a law of righteousness, did not arrive at that law. Why? Because they did not pursue it by faith, but as though it were by works. They stumbled over the stumbling stone" (Rom. 9:31-32 NASB). "Blindness in part is happened to Israel.... For God hath concluded them all in unbelief, that He might have mercy upon all" (Rom. 11:25,32).

Trouble, or the breaking up of our unfruitful or fallow ground, is designed to bring us to a place of despair from which we will call on God. This will result in hope! "Tribulation [trouble] worketh patience; and patience, experience; and experience, hope: and hope maketh not ashamed; because the love of God is shed abroad in our hearts..." (Rom. 5:3-5).

In fact, that door or gate (the removing of the veil) is found in place of trouble. God says, "I will...bring her into the wilderness.... I will give her...the valley of Achor [trouble] for a door of hope: and she shall sing there" (Hos. 2:14-15). The valley of Achor was the valley of trouble. It was there that they stoned Achan (see Josh. 7) because he "troubled Israel." It is in the time of trouble when we cry to the Lord for deliverance.

> *If I* [God] *shut up heaven that there be no rain, or if I command the locusts to devour the land, or if I send pestilence among My people; if My people...humble themselves, and pray, and seek My face, and turn from their wicked ways; then will I hear from heaven, and will forgive their sin, and will heal their land* (2 Chronicles 7:13-14).

My wife, Jeanne, and I experienced this "door of hope" open in our valley of trouble. As mentioned in the previous chapter, our youngest son, James, developed schizophrenia when he was about 16. The disease progressed rapidly, and he was hospitalized for months at a time, several times a year. We were devastated and without hope, for the prognosis was for more of the same and worse. We cried out, but nothing happened. Nobody knew how to minister to James or Jeanne and me, thus people just avoided us. The future looked very bleak.

James became totally paranoid. He couldn't stand being with people—not even his family. He had to sleep all day to avoid us; he only came up at night. He couldn't even watch television other than the odd cartoon. Any stimulus sent him into a panic attack. James even tried to commit suicide several times. There was no answer, no hope.

Then one morning, Jeanne was reading in the Bible when she came across the verse that stated, "The Lord will smite you with madness" (Deut. 28:28 NASB). Madness, insanity, schizophrenia! *What caused this curse?* was her first thought. She backed up to chapter 27 of Deuteronomy and found that this curse was a result of generational sins. If there is a place of entrance, then there is a place of exit. Jeanne started to ask for forgiveness for her ancestors back four generations as the Bible stated, and then broke off the curse over the family and our children. I did the same.

God responded by saying to me, "I have put James in his own Egypt (captivity). I will protect him there and later I will bring him through the wilderness into his land of promise (his destiny)." With us claiming that word, James started to improve immediately. He has not gone to the hospital since. He even graduated from high school. He started working short-term jobs with our company and got on a fairly regular schedule. He started making friends and doing activities. During this time, we sat down with the prophet, Bob Jones, and he spoke a prophetic word concerning James. He encouraged us to start pushing the devil back out of James' territory. Bob demonstrated this by slowly, over the course of five minutes, pushing a glass of water, a couple of inches at a time, across the table. He encouraged us to demand more territory in prayer even when we had gained a victory.

Then the miracles started occurring. People saw the change that was happening in our family. They wanted to know how to get that freedom and victory. So we started walking our friends through the cures we had found in the Bible. We delved deeper to see if we could find more curses blocking the blessings. Things started to grow, and we had to put all the principles down in a manual. People in the church got set free and wanted to be a part of what was happening. We developed a large ministry team to handle the seminars we were now doing.

At the time of the writing of this book, we have taken over 2,000 people through the course. We have presented this tool of freedom in Guatemala and Cuba, and others have taken it to Nicaragua and El Salvador. James has continued to improve and is even helping with the soundboard and with some of the television ministry at the church.

Someone once asked me, if I had a choice, would I go through it all again? I had to think: so much pain for James and ourselves, so many tears, so much hopelessness. Yet because of God and His love, both James and thousands of others have received freedom and liberty; so I had to admit, "Yes, I would do it all again." The sacrifice was worth it. God opened a door of hope in our valley of trouble, and no man could close it. That is the power of hope.

Jeremiah was even more dramatic in his portrayal of this principle that trouble produces hope. Jeremiah goes through 19 verses of misery, trouble, and anguish. He uses words like: *affliction… darkness…broken…bones…gall and travail…hedged about…pulled in pieces…made desolate…bitterness…wormwood…broken teeth… hope perished* (see Lam. 3:1-19). He then starts a shift in his spirit.

He declares, "My soul [has] them still in remembrance, and is humbled in me. This I recall to my mind, therefore have I *hope*" (Lam. 3:20-21). What a turnaround!

Jeremiah then goes on and declares God's goodness. "Mercies...compassions...new every morning: great is Thy faithfulness. The Lord is my portion...therefore will I hope.... It is good...[to] hope and quietly wait for the salvation of the Lord" (Lam. 3:22-24,26).

Hard circumstances will turn to hope if we don't harden ourselves against God. It is not our circumstances that God is trying to change, but our independent nature that He is trying to kill. God can change our circumstance in an instant. He took Joseph from being a slave in a foreign prison to being Prime Minister of Egypt in less than a day, but it took 17 years for Joseph to have his soul prepared for this time to be the savior of his people and Egypt. The process took so long because the calling was so high. It seems that Joseph's crowning achievement, as recorded in Hebrews, was not the faith it took to become the Prime Minister but the faith he displayed in prophesying that Israel would receive her promise of occupying the land Abraham had procured for her and that his own final resting place would be in it. "By faith Joseph, when he died, made mention of the departing of the children of Israel; and gave commandment concerning his bones" (Heb. 11:22).

That statement of faith was what God was impressed with: Joseph's believing and seeing the triumph of God's Kingdom plans and his determination to be part of it, even if he was dead! Egypt meant nothing. Anybody could be the Prime Minister. In fact, Joseph's nature was so altered that, when his brothers approached him tearfully, to plead for their lives, he cried and replied, "Fear not...am I in the place of God? [In a sense, he was; he had the power of life and death over them]...[you] thought evil against me; but God meant it [for] good...to save much people alive" (Gen. 50:19-20). The position and power meant nothing; the degradation and slavery also meant nothing. God's will and purpose, accomplished through trouble, was all that counted to Joseph.

Unlike Joseph, who submitted to God's purposes through hope when troubles came, we often harden our hearts. Instead of humbling ourselves and being broken and contrite as Joseph was, we get proud and fight against what God is doing. That fighting to keep from changing our hearts results in God's not being allowed to change our circumstances. The consequence of our rebellion is more blindness. "The pride of your heart has deceived you" (Obad. 3).

HARDENING

Pharaoh is the prime example of the hardening of a heart. He proudly announces his disregard and contempt for God and God's will. "Pharaoh said, Who is the Lord, that I should obey His voice to let Israel go? I know not the Lord, neither will I let Israel go" (Exod. 5:2). He drew the line in the sand and proudly declared his purposes. Then it began: a revelation of God's power started to unfold before Pharaoh's eyes, but his pride blinded him. "I will harden Pharaoh's heart, and multiply My signs...in the land of Egypt" (Exod. 7:3).

God worked with Pharaoh, knowing that the more he was pushed, the more he would resist. So God would push and then draw back, push and draw back, slowly allowing Pharaoh to fall into blindness. Here is an account of some of the plagues that came on Egypt and the responses of Pharaoh to them:

Frogs—"When Pharaoh saw that there was respite, he hardened his heart" (Exod. 8:15).

Lice—"Magicians said…This is the finger of God: and Pharaoh's heart was hardened" (Exod. 8:19).

Flies—"Pharaoh hardened his heart" (Exod. 8:32).

Murrain (a plague-like disease in cattle)—"Not one of the cattle of the Israelites [was] dead. And the heart of Pharaoh was hardened" (Exod. 9:7).

He was seeing but no longer perceiving.

Hail—"He that feared the word of the Lord among the servants of Pharaoh made his servants and his cattle flee into the houses: And he [Pharaoh] that regarded not the word of the Lord [saw it as nothing] left his…cattle in the field" (Exod. 9:20-21).

After dealing only with the circumstance (the plagues) and not his heart, Pharaoh stuck to his guns when things eased off. God knew just how far to push him without breaking the hardness. The principle is clear: if the circumstances change before we are changed, we will harden our hearts. *This is why we should never desire deliverance before brokenness. It is too dangerous. The battle went on.*

Then the hail "ceased...and [Pharaoh] hardened his heart, he and his servants" (Exod. 9:34). The pride and the stubbornness are now starting to spread to those he had authority over.

"The Lord said...I have hardened his heart, and the heart of his servants, that I might shew these My signs before him...that [you may] tell...thy son, and of thy son's son, what things I [did] in Egypt...that ye may know...that I am the Lord" (Exod. 10:1-2). The obedient ones (the Israelites) were starting to see God and His power. The disobedient ones (the Egyptians) were losing the ability to see (understand) anything that was going on. Finally a crack appears in the resistance of the proud leaders of Egypt.

Locusts—"Pharaoh's servants said...Let the men go.... Do you not yet know that Egypt is destroyed?" (Exod. 10:7 NKJV). The pressure of the trouble has started to make them look for some hope of relief, but Pharaoh is still choosing to be blind.

Death Angel—The last plague caused a breaking. "Pharaoh rose...and there was a great cry in Egypt...not a house where there was not one dead" (Exod. 12:30). Pharaoh finally broke and humbled himself and let the people go, but just as before, because his heart had not been changed, blindness and hardness descended one last time.

"I will harden Pharaoh's heart...that the Egyptians may know that I am the Lord. ...And the heart of Pharaoh and of his servants was turned...and they said, 'Why have we done this, that we have let Israel go from serving us?'" (Exod. 14:4-5). Reading that makes me want to say to them, "Give your head a shake. You did this to save your own life." God just displayed awesome power, judgment, and mercy, and now they can't figure it out anymore. This is ultimate blindness.

For those who will humble themselves, trouble is a door of hope; for the proud, it is a door to disaster. The Egyptians continued to be so blinded to what was right in front of them—the pillar of smoke and fire, the Red Sea parting—that, seeking revenge, they blindly charged into the midst of the sea. There was absolutely no comprehension of the display of God's majesty that was right before their faces. Amazing!

This will happen again at the very end of the age because there will always be those who don't want God to rule over them. Even after Jesus has ruled on the earth for 1,000 years, when nature has been changed, when life has been lengthened, and a veritable paradise has flourished, satan will still be able to deceive people. The deception will be accomplished because of blindness that will exist even then. *Situations don't dictate responses; hearts do.* "When the thousand years are expired, Satan shall be loosed...and shall...deceive the nations...to gather them together to battle" (Rev. 20:7-8).

All this blindness occurs because we don't want to see. "When one turns [repents] to the Lord, the veil is taken away" (2 Cor. 3:16 NKJV). However, the deception remains when there is no turning. We may cry and ask forgiveness for what we have done, but if our hearts are not humbled, then we are only sorry for the consequences of our sin, not for how we have wounded Jesus or others. We are only sorry for ourselves. We only want our circumstances to change, not our hearts. That is a sure sign of an unrepentant heart, and it always leads to blindness.

I know a man who operated as a prophet who is in this very situation. He had a deep wound that he wasn't willing to deal with. This affected his ability to function in intimacy with his wife, so he left her. The churches were more interested in his gift than they were in him, so they continued to use him rather than try to heal him. This wound allowed satan to get a hook of lust in him, and he molested some girls.

I visited him in jail, and we talked. He wanted out of there and wanted his ministry restored. He wasn't thinking about anybody but himself and how he could get out of his troubles. I suggested that he humble himself, write to his wife and the girls he had molested, asking their forgiveness, plead guilty to the charges, and ask God for justice to be done. This would be the fruit of true repentance, and then God could show mercy. He didn't want justice; he just wanted the mercy so he could get out of jail, out of his circumstances.

We can exhibit pride, and God can humble us; or we can humble ourselves and let God exalt us. God is much better at what He does than we are! This man could not see what was happening and could not repent; he could only regret what he had done. He had lost his hope in the transforming power of the cross. He eventually pleaded guilty to some of the charges and served his sentence, but has yet to be restored to his wife or his ministry.

How do we tell the difference between repentance and regret? By our fruit! Jesus said, "You will know them by their fruits"

(Matt. 7:16 NKJV). It is not enough just to hear the Word; we must "be doers of the word, and not hearers only, deceiving yourselves" (James 1:22 NKJV). This deception, blindness, and hardening of the heart is a deep hole. The real problem is that we don't know how deep. Unless someone shines a light down this hole, we can't tell if it is 2 feet or 200 feet deep. This is the condition of our hearts. Jeremiah said, "The heart is deceitful...and desperately wicked: who can know it?" (Jer. 17:9).

The story of Esau and Jacob is a case in point. God chose Jacob and rejected Esau even in the womb. On what basis was this choice made? By election: God knew beforehand how they would react. Jacob would change, as indicated by his new name: Israel, but Esau would not. God was not playing with them; He was just being God, knowing what they would do because He could see their hearts. "Esau, who for one morsel of meat sold his birthright. ...Afterward...he found no place of repentance [no way to change his mind], though he sought it carefully with tears" (Heb. 12:16-17).

Part of our ability to see is our willingness to allow God to shine His light in us. The true light is seeing ourselves against the standard or plumb line of Jesus. Next to others, we may appear good, but next to God, we are a mess. The attitude of "I am better than others" never reveals the hardness or blindness in our own hearts.

THE HEART

We are told to judge ourselves that we should not be judged. A sign of lack of that self-judgment is the habit of judging others. "For wherein thou judgest another, thou condemnest thyself; for thou that judgest dost the same things" (Rom. 2:1). When God first said that verse to me, I thought, "No way! I don't do those things."

But God said, "Yes, you do."

I protested, "No, I don't!"

"Yes, you do."

Arguing with God should have been a sign of blindness, but I couldn't see it (I wonder why). Then God revealed the state of my heart. He showed me that I could only recognize in others those things that were also in me. Our sins are reflected in others! Other people are designed to be your mirror. The world knows this and says, "It takes a thief to know one." If you do not have a propensity toward a particular sin, you can't see it in others. (Now you may disagree with this statement, but please read on to see how this is true.) "Unto the pure all things are pure: but unto them that are defiled and unbelieving is nothing pure; but even their mind and conscience is defiled" (Titus 1:15).

This is why some people can get sucked into a scam. They can't comprehend anyone deliberately deceiving them because they would never do that to someone else. We call people like this naïve, but really they are just pure in this area. You may protest, as I did, that you have never committed a homosexual act or participated in an abortion, so how, God, can You say I am guilty of these things?

Earlier we read Second Chronicles 7:14, which talks about humbling ourselves to cleanse the land. A hardhearted person is proud and thus blind. A humble person can see his faults. God started to remove my pride in the fact that I didn't have this or that particular fruit in my life. God is not interested in pruning bad fruit. The Holy Spirit calls for something more drastic than just cutting off a little fruit. Jesus said, in paraphrase, "Bring forth fruit worthy of repentance and don't say you have Abraham as your father, for I say to you that God is able of the stones to raise up children unto Abraham" (see Matt. 3:8-9).

He is saying, "Don't think you are righteous just because you have a past history of seeming righteousness, but rather bring forth fruit by repenting." God is not looking at simple pruning but at going to the root. "Now the ax is laid to the root of the trees" (Matt. 3:10 NKJV). If we prune a tree, it will only bear more and stronger of the same fruit. That is why God prunes good trees and chops down bad. We on the other hand want to prune bad trees and leave the good ones alone.

God started to talk to me about why people get involved with abortion or homosexuality. What are the roots? Let's take abortion as the example.

> Most aborted babies were conceived in an atmosphere of lust.

> God said, "Did you ever act out of lust?"

> Young parents might say things like: "I can't afford this baby."

> Did you ever decide *not* to do what God wanted because of financial worries?

> "This is not convenient."

Ever make a poor choice because it wasn't convenient to do what was right?

"My boyfriend says, 'Me or the baby!'"

Ever act out of fear of rejection?

"This will hurt my career/body."

Ever act selfishly?

"What will people think?"

Ever not obey the truth to avoid ridicule?

We have done all those things, so we can't say, "I don't know how they could do such things" when we know very well how—because we do them too. Only the degree or particular manifestation of the fruit is different. The root is the same! That is why we can see it. Judgment against others then is evidence of blindness, which is itself indicative of pride (an unrealistic view of ourselves). In fact, the Bible says, if you "judge...you are not a doer...but a judge" (James 4:11 NKJV).

People then respond in two ways as a judge: "...their conscience also bearing witness and their thoughts the mean while *accusing* or else *excusing* one another" (Rom. 2:15). Even while feeling guilty for what is done, we will either accuse (judge) or excuse (justify) rather than intercede and exhort (encourage). Sin does not evaporate. We must deal with it. The cross is the only remedy to sin, but we must bring it there—both their sin and ours.

The opposite of blindness, of course, is sight or discernment. As stated earlier, the veil keeps us from seeing God, thus being able to properly judge ourselves by using Jesus as our plumb line. Going through the veil in the Bible was synonymous with bringing proper discernment. The priests were allowed through the veil on specific occasions. God said, "They shall come near...to minister unto Me" (Ezek. 44:15). After coming into God's presence, God said they could, "Teach My people the difference between the holy and profane, and cause them to discern between unclean and the clean" (Ezek. 44:23).

The only true discernment comes from being in God's presence. It is not just the ability to hear or not hear, but also the degree to which we hear that is important. Information is power. So our ability to hear from God, the ultimate source of information, depends on our willingness to go through whatever veils our hearts and minds.

"Then came there a voice from heaven.... The people [who] heard it, said that it thundered: others said, An angel spake to him" (John 12:28-29). Some heard God speak. Some thought an angel spoke. Some only heard thunder. Same sound; different discernment. The degree of the people's commitment to Jesus determined what they could hear. Some couldn't commit because "they loved the praise of men more than the praise of God" (John 12:43). They were incapable of seeing past what was in their faces. Their minds could not comprehend that there was more than what they could think. They had no hope for more; but there is more.

"Eye [has] not seen, nor ear heard, neither [has it] entered into the heart of man, the things which God [has] prepared for them that love Him" (1 Cor. 2:9). This is our hope. There is more than we see, more than our situations suggest. We have to be able to hear and to believe what we hear.

John the Baptist had heard God speak from Heaven concerning Jesus as God's Son, but now he was in prison. He had expected that he would be part of the coming kingdom that he "knew" was about to be set up. Now it seemed his hope was fading. He was offended that Jesus had not gotten him out of prison (see Matt. 11:6). Jesus had to say, "Go and [show] John *again*" (Matt. 11:4). John had lost hope because he got offended and now doubted what he already knew. It cost him his life.

Even the disciples lost hope after the death of Jesus. Two of them said to Jesus on the road to Emmaus, "We were hoping that it was He who was going to redeem Israel" (Luke 24:21 NKJV)—this after watching all the miracles and hearing all His wisdom! But now, because they had lost hope, they had lost all the power in which they had operated through faith. They were operating in fear and hiding behind locked doors: "The doors were shut...for fear of the Jews" (John 20:19). They had lost hope and thus had lost vision and power.

Paul and Silas were in a similar situation: in prison, beaten, and denied justice, but they had a different response. "At midnight Paul and Silas prayed, and sang praises.... And suddenly there was a great earthquake...all the doors opened, and every one's bands [chains] were loosed" (Acts 16:25-26). Now that is power. They were able to exercise it because they had heard a word to come to this city and were able to, in hope, hang onto that word, knowing the word had power over the situation. This hope will protect your mind and your ability to see and hear. Let us daily put on "as a helmet the hope of salvation" (1 Thess. 5:8 NKJV).

We don't have to be perfect. God loves imperfect vessels. "We have this treasure in earthen vessels, that the excellency of the power may be of God, and not of us" (2 Cor. 4:7). We are, however, responsible to operate in faith, hope, and love. It is "Christ in you, the hope of glory" (Col. 1:27). "Now abide faith, hope, and love" (1 Cor. 13:13 NKJV).

The world's hope is wishful thinking: "I hope it doesn't rain"; "I hope I get a job"; etc. It is always directed to the future but has no power to affect the future. Christian hope is based on what Jesus already accomplished on the cross, "according to His abundant mercy hath begotten us...unto a lively hope by the resurrection of Jesus" (1 Pet. 1:3) and has power to change our circumstances.

Knowing all this, "let us lay aside every weight, and the sin which [does] so easily beset us, and let us run...the race that is set before us" (Heb. 12:1) and operate in authority and power through "Christ Jesus, who is our hope" (1 Tim. 1:1 NASB).

ENDNOTE

1. At the time of writing, Karen is close to term with a second child, a boy.

Chapter 4

When God, When? — Patience and Rest

Hang on. Have patience. God is not slow; it only seems that way. It was raining when Jeanne picked up the kids from her friend's house, located in a rural part of our county. A road construction crew had just set up their barricades, which forced Jeanne to take the detour route. A few cars were ahead of her on this twisty little road that wound through the hills near a ski resort. The locals called this glorified cow path "the Coyote Trail." The road had not been maintained and, with the rain, had become slippery and rutted.

Jeanne crept along at about ten miles per hour, following the line of cars in front of her. The vehicle directly in front of her was having problems with traction and finally got stuck. Jeanne was driving a big van with lots of traction, so she offered to give him a little push. She managed to get him going, only to have to repeat the process several times. The rest of the cavalcade had long since disappeared before Jeanne finally got back to a main road, about 20 minutes later. The gentleman she had been pushing got out and thanked her for her help. Just as he was turning to walk back to his car, he asked, "Is this the road to Edmonton?"

Jeanne was surprised and snickered, "You didn't have to go down this road at all. Edmonton is the other way. You turned the wrong way at the detour. Edmonton is east, and you have been heading west." She left him standing by his car pondering his options.

Part of the process for making right decisions is to start from the right premise. This poor man had made a wrong turn and went through a treacherous ordeal simply because he came to a conclusion based on his own perceptions of how to get to where he was going.

We too can come to the wrong conclusion if we start from the wrong foundational truth. God has created the visible world to explain the invisible, unseen realm. "The invisible things of Him...are clearly seen, being understood by the things that are made" (Rom. 1:20). The processes of nature are designed to give us the keys to understanding the operation of the Kingdom of God and the natural occurrences in our own lives. We shouldn't think that we can change the natural course of things just because we don't like the process.

God's response to Noah's first offering after the flood was that He would not bring complete catastrophe on the earth anymore, but rather "seedtime and harvest, and cold and heat, and summer and winter, and day and night shall not cease" (Gen. 8:22). God established the seasons and times that would govern the cycles on the earth. There is always time between sowing and harvesting. In our modern world, if we want some potatoes, we just go to the store and buy some potatoes. If we want strawberries, we do the same.

When my grandfather wanted potatoes, he had to plant them and wait until they grew. This need to grow their food forced people into planning ahead so that there would be sufficient provisions in storage for the winter. Growing things took time, and you had to literally "make hay while the sun shone." If you had no hay stored up, you would be in trouble over the winter. Your animals might die and so might you. I believe Jeremiah had a similar thing in mind when he said, "The harvest is past, the summer is ended, and we are not saved" (Jer. 8:20). We are not separated from the consequences of natural seasons just because we don't grow our own food. The seasons still affect us.

We must learn to recognize the seasons we are in. Jesus found it hard to believe that the Jewish people of His day could "discern the face of the sky, but [could not] discern the signs of the times" (Matt. 16:3 NKJV). God expects us to look around and see what is happening, especially in our own lives. When Jeanne and I were younger and had little kids, we could not function like we can now. There were different priorities, with

131

the family being the major one. We got a phone call late one night from someone who needed deliverance. However, Jeanne was breast-feeding and was not feeling like entering into spiritual warfare, so we said no. Someone else in the Body would have to carry that load. That was not selfishness; it was right priorities for the season. The Bible even commands that a newly married couple be free from all responsibilities for one year (see Deut. 24:5).

This acknowledgment of seasons will remove the pressure from us always needing to see results. A farmer does not expect a harvest during seedtime; neither does he expect growth during winter. Jeanne and I have been able to sow financially above the tithe in faith because we knew that when the time was ripe our seeds would become mature fruit. As a result, we have had authority to call in the harvest when God said it was time. Understanding the seasons in corporate settings often requires God to speak in a more dramatic fashion.

Jeanne had a prophetic dream several years ago. In the dream she saw a man and was given his name. When she awoke, she could only remember the first name: Marc. She knew the last name was French but couldn't quite recall it. God prompted her to ask a friend if he was aware of anybody by that first name. He mentioned some people he knew, and Jeanne recognized one as the name she heard in the dream: Brisebois. She called this complete stranger's home in Vancouver and left a message on his phone describing the dream.

Marc listened to the message, but not knowing who Jeanne was, he did not respond. Later, through a chance meeting with a mutual friend in Ontario, God confirmed that the dream was from Him. Marc phoned, and two days later he was sitting in our living room discussing the dream and what God was saying. God was shifting our church's emphasis back to its original calling. Marc was to be a major part of that shift, and through a series of remarkable events, he became our pastor. The dream assisted the leadership in discerning the season the Lord was taking us into.

Knowing the times can allow us to rest while others are fretting. Jeremiah was told to not "take a wife, nor...have sons or daughters" (Jer. 16:2 NKJV) in Jerusalem. God said they would all die, and He wanted to save Jeremiah the grief of their loss. Jeremiah was also told not to seek glory because trouble was coming, and it would all be a wasted effort.

If I had listened to the Lord on that point, I would have saved myself a lot of grief. Earlier in my life, I poured all my effort and hopes into what my flesh desired, which was to gain wealth and position. Had I sought God for His direction first, I would not have had to suffer seeing my dreams dissolve into nothing. All the authority I had accumulated, through my self-effort, evaporated overnight when I fell out of favor with the companies on which I had hung my star. Ambition is a characteristic of the flesh, but "fleshly lusts...war against the soul" (1 Pet. 2:11) and bring no spiritual fruit. On the other hand, seeds that God sows have "fruit that remains" (see John 15:16).

Jim Elliot, a missionary who was martyred, once said, "He is no fool, who gives what he cannot keep, to gain that which he cannot lose."[1] Knowing the season allows us to have patience and to stop striving. The opposite is also true. God wanted the

Jews to marry, raise children, and build houses in their captivity because they were going to be there 70 years (see Jer. 29:5-10). Even in Jerusalem, after the city was captured, the residents were told to buy land and seal the deeds because they would need them later, when God brought them back from captivity (see Jer. 32:14-20). God understands how to create wealth through the real estate cycle: buy and build during the bad times, sell during the good. If we can listen to God, rather than our own reasoning, we can go with His flow; if not, we will always be swimming upstream.

The Jews, it seemed, were always out of sync with what was happening. God was declaring destruction by Babylon; they were declaring victory. When the season of judgment shifted to a season of mercy, God told them to stay in the land, to not go to Egypt, and to not fear Babylon; but they decided to flee. There was no discernment of what God was doing because, as mentioned before, there was no intention to obey, surrender, and trust. Even in Jesus' time, the Jews still missed their season (see Luke 19:41-42). If we try to resist or rebuke the seasons that God has ordained, we will not have success and indeed will be found fighting God.

Gamaliel, during the disciples' time, counseled the Sanhedrin concerning the Christians. "If this counsel or this work be of men, it will come to [nothing]: But if it be of God, [you] cannot overthrow it; lest [unfortunately you] be found even to fight against God" (Acts 5:38-39). The problem for us is that everything from God and every new move of God always appears in seed form, which, as with most seeds, does not look like the mature fruit. Jesus said that we would know them (people) by their fruit, not their seeds. It takes time for seeds to mature sufficiently to properly identify what fruit it is.

In the parable of the tares, Jesus instructed the angels to wait until seeds had matured before separating them. They asked, "'[Shall we] go and gather them up?'...'Nay, lest while you gather up the tares, ye root up also the wheat with them'" (Matt. 13:28-29). Too often a quick judgment has uprooted that which would have been a fruitful seed. Jesus states that understanding the parable of the sower and the seed was vital for understanding the mysteries of the Kingdom. "Unto you it is given to know the mystery of the kingdom.... Know [you] not this parable? And how then will [you understand] all parables?" (Mark 4:11,13).

Understanding the nature of maturity will allow us to properly comprehend the nature of growth. Today everything is instantaneous. There are instant lottery millionaires, fast food or microwave food, and nearly instant travel around the world. Growth, however, is not instantaneous; it is a process. That is why a novice is not to be granted a place of governance in a church (see 1 Tim. 3:6). Authority over demons came as a right, instantaneously after being saved and brought into the Kingdom. "Those who believe: In My name they will cast out demons" (Mark 16:17 NKJV). Authority (leadership) over people required maturity and a servant's heart. This heart takes time to develop: "first the blade, then the ear, after that the full corn in the ear" (Matt. 4:28).

Part of maturity is the ability to bear weight, the willingness to take responsibility, especially for our own faults and sins. There is a difference between being evil and being immature. The two may appear the same, but God sees the heart. We have a hard time discerning the difference because all we can see is the fruit. As long as there is growth, there will be immaturity. Wheat, when it is in the leaf or just headed out, is immature, but it is 100 percent pure wheat. Purity is not maturity, and maturity is not purity. Evil will also mature (see Matt.13:30). Jesus enjoyed living with immaturity; so can we. That's why kids are so much fun; they are immature. If the Church was more like a family, we wouldn't mind the kids acting immature; we might even like it. The disciples displayed their lack of maturity in the middle of demonstrations of power, and Jesus still loved them. God can see where we are going, but that is not why He can enjoy us.

He enjoys us because He loves us. "God demonstrates His own love towards us, in that while we were still sinners, Christ died for us" (Rom. 5:8 NKJV). God loves us because we are His children, not because we perform properly. On just one walk, Jesus had to give His disciples three rebukes concerning pride and ambition, (see Luke 9:46-48), territorialism, (see Luke 9:49-50), and harsh judgment (see Luke 9:53-56). I would have sent these guys back to Bible school or seminary to get their attitudes adjusted before I would have allowed them any more opportunities to minister, but Jesus was not fazed. He was looking at their hearts, which were pure, not at their actions, which were immature. We can see His confidence in them by the fact that He immediately appointed 70 more disciples (see Luke 10:1) who had not, until this time, even made the cut. He was saying by this action, "I like these guys. I need more just like them." The seed (the word of God) and the soil (their hearts) were both pure and full of the life necessary to produce a crop. The only thing lacking was the right atmosphere (their thought patterns or attitudes). As I have heard Rick Joyner say, "Anything worth doing is worth doing poorly." You will never learn to walk until you walk poorly. You will never learn to talk until you talk poorly. The children of immigrants learn to speak a new language much faster than their parents because they are not concerned about how they sound or if they make a mistake. God loves that childlike attitude and states that unless we are "…converted [change the way we think][2], and become as little children, [we] shall not enter into the kingdom of heaven (Matt. 18:3). God loves us just the way we are, but He loves us too much to leave us just the way we are.

Jesus gave them power and authority over demons and diseases (see Luke 9:1). They received revelation, "[You are] the Christ of God" (Luke 9:20). Then they heard God speak from Heaven: "And a voice came out of the cloud, saying, 'This is My beloved Son…'" (Luke 9:35 NKJV). Even though they were in the middle of all that was happening in the Kingdom, they demonstrated their immaturity time and again. Pride rose up. "Then a dispute arose among them as to which of them would be greatest" (Luke 9:46 NKJV). Arrogance showed its ugly head. "We saw someone casting out demons in Your name, and we forbade him because he does not follow with us" (Luke 9:49 NKJV). Finally a murdering spirit revealed itself. "[Should] we command fire to come down from heaven and consume them" (Luke 9:54).

All this was going on in the most mature group of disciples. What was Jesus' reaction to their display of fleshy responses?

"This is good, I need more guys just like you, doing the work." "After these things the Lord appointed seventy [more]" (Luke 10:1 NKJV). And He was excited with the results. "I beheld Satan as lightning fall from heaven" (Luke 10:18). You might think that the disciples were immature, but they had an intimate relationship with God and had power in prayer. Really? It was after this display of power that they asked, "Lord, teach us to pray" (Luke 11:1). At that point Jesus gave them the "Lord's Prayer."

They were raw recruits who believed they could do it because Jesus said they could, but they were not ready to rule in the Kingdom; that would take pruning to remove their flesh. God says that He will prune every fruitful tree and lay the ax to every unfruitful root. This is a lifelong process. Even in Heaven, it seems that God is still maturing the saints, for we still hear that cry, "How long, O Lord...dost Thou not judge and avenge? ...Rest yet for a little season, until their fellowservants also and their brethren [death's]...should be fulfilled" (Rev. 6:10-11).

It takes a season to allow fruit to ripen or for judgment and deliverance to come. *Purity is not maturity.* The smallest blade of wheat is 100 percent pure wheat, but it cannot reproduce. *Maturity is not purity.* Mature weeds can reproduce, but they are zero percent wheat. We must have patience and rest until the Father matures us enough to reproduce the image of His Son in us.

Anything we would reproduce before we are pure and mature in spirit would be from our mature flesh. God knows how long this process or season will take. The Jewish nation had to go into captivity (a place to grow) for 400 years in Egypt because "the iniquity of the Amorites is not yet full" (Gen.

15:16). Jesus Himself waited until "the fullness of the time" (Gal. 4:4 NKJV) before He came. Power and authority is released when we know how to rest and cooperate with God in these seasons.

Just prior to New Year's Eve 2000, our son James, who has schizophrenia, had a crisis with fear attacking him. As the new millennium approached, satan was tormenting James with thoughts that he was going to kill him in the New Year. A couple of days after Christmas, the paranoia came to a head. James became very upset and insisted that he needed to go to the hospital. We had been down this road before, and I knew the outcome: sitting for several hours in an emergency ward, then getting sent home because there was nobody to admit him and there were no beds in the psych ward. James became more insistent, and Jeanne went upstairs to pray so she wouldn't have to witness the battle. I was trying to reason with James but was getting nowhere. "God, what do I do," I pleaded.

A quiet voice spoke into my ear the words, "Evil Foreboding." I silently bound a spirit of evil foreboding and then asked God to give James clarity. Immediately he calmed down and stopped yelling at me. I challenged him to repent of his fear for certain situations that had upset him and to renounce his words of doom. To my surprise he cooperated and repented. I then got him to go after the spirit of "Evil Foreboding" and command it to go. Again to my surprise, James cooperated and did everything I told him to. Then he casually said, "I'm kind of hungry, Dad. Let's talk about this later." He then grabbed a snack from the fridge and went upstairs. I stood in the kitchen stunned. Five minutes before, James and I were in the middle of a raging spiritual battle, and now he was calmly having a snack. I knew we had entered a new season.

God also uses time to mature or build character. Some of that maturity of character is the ability to recognize our own weakness and our inability to obtain what God promised. Jeanne had to mature in order to conquer the fears that kept her locked up in our house. For a while she was not able to go visit a neighbor or even go out of the house for fear a neighbor would see her and want to talk. She had a hard time going to the mall by herself. Now she flies all over the country by herself and enjoys speaking before large audiences.

Part of maturity is experience. The more times God proves His goodness and protection, the easier it is to trust Him. I had to mature in trust also, so that I could rest and not always strive. I used to be very performance-oriented, which really is just a fear that I won't be accepted unless I work for it. This is a manifestation of an orphan spirit. God has been delivering me of this inability to be a son and to receive an inheritance instead of working for wages.

Our God is a covenant-making God. Some of His covenants, God made with Himself because He knew we weren't ready or able to fulfill our part. In Genesis 15, Abraham asked God, "How shall I know that I will inherit it?" (Gen. 15:8 NKJV). God gave Abraham instructions on how to prepare a sacrifice and how to arrange the carcasses after he had split them. This had all the appearances of being part of a ceremony for making a covenant. Normally both of the participants in the covenant would pass between the pieces to initiate the process but only a "smoking furnace, and a burning lamp…passed between the pieces" (Gen. 15:17). Abraham himself, as one of the covenant partners, wasn't asked to pass through! God manifested Himself in two symbolic forms and made the covenant with Himself. "For when God made promise to Abraham, because He could swear by no greater, He [swore] by Himself, saying, "…I will bless…I will multiply thee" (Heb. 6:13-14).

What was Abraham's part? "And so, after he had patiently endured, he obtained the promise" (Heb. 6:15). All he had to do was to rest and patiently endure. The process is: *receive the Promise, endure the Problem, obtain the Provision.* With each promise, we will have a problem, but our problem isn't the problem. Our problem is that we don't have the character to operate at the higher spiritual plane, which walking in the promise requires. Our character is developed in a desert—which is exactly the opposite in appearance of the promise, and likely even worse than the place we were before receiving the promise. The children of Israel immediately experienced this principle when Pharaoh made them find their own straw after Moses prophesied their release from captivity. How did they respond?

Promise—"The people believed…they bowed…and worshipped" (Exod. 4:31). They thought this would be great.

Problem—"[Lord,] look…and judge; because [You] have made our savour to [stink…and] put a sword in their hand to slay us" (Exod. 5:21). Pharaoh reacted and made their life worse, so now they were mad. This was not what Moses had promised. He had promised milk and honey, and now they just had more work.

They were judging the wrong person. They were mad at Moses and God, who were trying to deliver them. Pharaoh was the enemy. Their reaction exposed their immaturity.

Provision—God's reply was: "Now you shall see what I do" (Exod. 6:1 NKJV).

The process had begun! Because the Israelites accepted the promise, a bargain (a covenant) was struck. It's like deciding to go on a roller coaster. It looks like it will be fun, but once it starts, the realization that you are no longer in control and cannot get off sets in, and fear begins to take over. The first drop is a sign of worse things to come, and the screaming starts. The whole point of riding a roller coaster, of course, is to use the momentum of the drop to propel you to the next level—God has a similar goal. A diagram may help see the process:

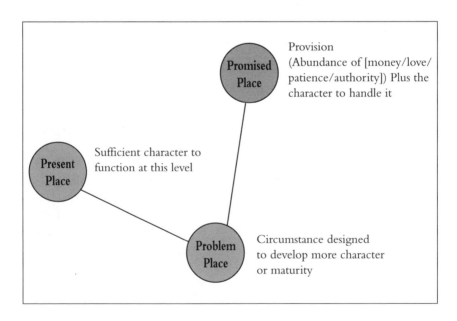

Problems Develop Character

The way down is the way up. Israel's response—murmuring and complaining—to the problem should have been a sure indication to them of their lack of character in believing what God said. Their emotions of anger, fear, resentment, and bitterness showed that they had more faith in satan's (Pharaoh's) abilities to affect them than they did in God's abilities to deliver them. God wasn't deterred by their screaming display of protest. It was too late. While the Israelites were wondering how far this was going to go, God had already told them, "Just watch Me."

Over the next few weeks, God sent them on a ride that none of them could have imagined. The fear, the exhilaration, the awe was all designed not to change their circumstances (that was guaranteed by God's word) but their character—their ability to trust God that when He says something, it will happen, no matter what it looks like.

Unfortunately for that generation, the ride was too scary (that is, they allowed fear to have a foothold), and even though they survived and got out of Egypt, they weren't ready to make it a lifestyle. They died in the wilderness, which was designed to be the conduit that would get them into the Promised Land. Hebrews says, "They could not enter in because of unbelief" (Heb. 3:19). "Let us therefore fear, lest, a promise...of entering into His rest...you should...come short of" (Heb. 4:1).

Just as they had a Promised Land, so we have a land of promises; to enter it we must come to a state of rest and patiently wait for God to work it out for us. Unfortunately we often try to do the working out. We can't do it. If we could, the promise wouldn't be from God. He is the only one who can fulfill His own word. "For he that is entered into His rest…[has] ceased from his own works, as God did from His" (Heb. 4:10).

Rest—no more work
Work—no more rest
} Your Choice

The problem is that it is difficult to maintain our state of rest when everything is falling down around us in the wilderness. There is a poignant joke that states, "If you can maintain your cool while all those around you are losing theirs, you obviously don't understand the problem." That is how the world sees rest; it does not make sense. Their philosophy often is: "When in worry or in doubt, run in circles, scream and shout."

God is removing all our dependence on our flesh, and it is humiliating. The abasing that occurs during these panic times drives out our pride, our fear of what people think, our trust in our own abilities, our independence, our judgment of others, and even our ambitions. I remember quitting a job once to work closer to home. I took a position as the steel erection foreman building a dragline. This was a job that I had really wanted, and I was in my glory.

After a few months the construction superintendent called me in and sat me down. He asked me if I would like to take over the layout and the fabrication on the job because they didn't have anybody else who was qualified to do the work accurately. Dragline construction requires precise layout and measuring, which were skills I possessed.

I replied that he had hired me to be the foreman on the erection crew, and if he wanted me to do the layout, I would be willing, but I would still want the foreman's rate. Now it got interesting.

"No, I can't justify that," the supervisor replied. "But I need you to take this job. Foremen are a dime a dozen, but a good fitter is hard to find."

I wanted to quit; I was so mad. Then God started to talk to me about my reactions. "Why had I taken this job?" I had come to be close to home. I had left another foreman's job to come, but the travel time here made up for the loss of wages. I knew God was dealing with my pride and my greed, so I humbled myself and took the fitter's job.

Paul said, in paraphrase, "I have learned to abound and to be abased, satisfied in whatever state I find myself" (see Phil. 4:12). How could he have that attitude? He knew God was in control and was willing to rest in that knowledge. Jesus Himself, when defending His healing of a lame man, said, "My Father has been working until now, and [therefore] I have been working" (John 5:17 NKJV). "The Son can do nothing of Himself [His own initiative], but what He sees the Father do; for whatever He does, the Son also does in like manner" (John 5:19 NKJV). Jesus wasn't into works. He was into God, and the works flowed out of His love not His striving.

Jesus chided the Ephesian church on their priorities: "I know your works...labor...patience...for My name's sake... and [you] have not become weary. Nevertheless...you have left your first love...repent" (Rev. 2:2-5 NKJV). Even patience, if it is not done for love, doesn't profit, and it doesn't change our character. Independence is a characteristic that has a hard time obeying and indicates striving and not rest.

Sacrifice is also a substitute for obedience. Sacrifice is works: my work, my labor, my striving, but always because I don't want to do it God's way. Cults and false religion exist because people don't want to come in contact with God themselves and be changed. They want to change their circumstances, the government, others' morality, or actions that affect them, but not change themselves. This is work; it takes constant effort and does not merit God's approval. He is more interested in what we are than in what we do. "He that is slow to anger is better than the mighty; and he that [rules] his spirit than he that [takes] a city" (Prov. 16:32). This was the reason for the rebuke to the church at Ephesus—because constant working and striving to do what is right distracts us from the real reason we exist. The first and greatest commandment is to love the Lord with all your soul and all your strength and all your mind.

He doesn't want us to work for Him; He wants to work through us. To do that we need to be one with God as Jesus was. You cannot work His works unless you can think His thoughts. That takes quality time—every day in every situation looking for Him to act, so that we can act in concert.

David learned this early. "David enquired again of God; and God said...Come upon them over against the mulberry trees. ...When [you hear] a sound of going in the tops of the mulberry trees...then thou shalt go out to battle: for God is gone forth before [you] to smite…the Philistines" (1 Chron. 14:14-15). God goes to war; we go to war. God rests; we rest.

I had a hard time learning this. I was so anxious to succeed that when I saw a good opportunity to invest, I just took it. It took too long to wait for God; I just didn't have the patience. Several disasters later, I am finding that acting in haste and repenting at my leisure is no fun. I am finally breaking my confidence in my flesh. I know that God's ideas always work. The house we are now living in took three months of patient silence to obtain, as you read earlier. It was actually easy, as I had already started the process. The secret of painless waiting is to let things die. We must lose our fleshly desire and just trust that God will bring better things into our lives than we could create ourselves. If we can do that, we won't run ahead of Him; we'll just go along for the ride.

Mary and Martha are examples of rest versus labor. Martha wanted Jesus to chide Mary for not working enough; but Jesus said Mary had chosen the better part, which was to sit at Jesus' feet. Mary had the heart that Jesus loved. When it came time for Jesus to do something for them—raise Lazarus—it is interesting to see His different responses to them.

With Martha, He tried to raise her vague faith to now faith, today's faith. Martha had faith for yesterday, "If You had been here, my brother would not have died" (John 11:21 NKJV); faith for tomorrow, "I know that he will rise…at the last day" (John 11:24 NKJV); but no faith for today. Jesus said, "'Take away the stone.' Martha…said to Him, 'Lord…[he stinks] for he has been dead four days'" (John 11:39 NKJV). She couldn't see the way out of today's problem.

Mary also was hopeless, but she could touch God's heart because she had decided to simply rest at His feet. When Jesus saw her weeping, "He groaned in [His] spirit" (John 11:33). Her resting moved Him to action, and He changed the circumstances. Martha got a teaching on resurrection; Mary got a resurrection. We also can make that happen if we can only rest.

God is always trying to show us our hearts so we can see what He wants to kill and resurrect in us. But "the heart is deceitful...who can know it?" (Jer. 17:9). So God gives us a promise, a word about what He is going to do. That word then starts to reveal what is in our hearts. "For the word of God is quick, and powerful, and sharper than any twoedged sword, piercing even to the dividing asunder of soul and spirit, and of the joints and marrow, and is a discerner of the thoughts and intents of the heart" (Heb. 4:12).

In the long run, the word is more about what God wants to do *in* you, rather than *for* or *through* you. The sacrifice, in the Old Testament, was to be divided at the joints so as not to break any bones. One part would be for God (to be burnt on the altar), another part for the priest, and another part for the dunghill. So it is with us: the dividing in us is between what is soulish and what is spiritual, thus revealing the real thoughts and intents (motivations) of our heart.

God knows what it takes to make us respond. He wants us to cooperate. That is why we are told, "present your bodies a living sacrifice...be transformed by the renewing of your mind, that you may prove what is that good and acceptable and perfect will of God" (Rom. 12:1-2 NKJV). He wants us to cooperate and not be like a horse or mule in whose mouth He has to put a bit.

The same word can go to two people but have different results. To one who resists change, the word will cause him to be hardened. To another who is yielded, the word will cause him to break and ask for mercy. *Transformation is a slow process. It always starts with the mouth.* We need to talk ourselves into changing. We need to encourage our own souls.

If we change our speaking:

   ...we will affect the way we think,

   ...our words will influence our emotions or our feelings,

   ...our feelings will cause us to act,

   ...our actions will dictate our habits,

   ...our habits will constitute our character,

   ...and our character will move us into our destiny.

We are all headed somewhere, but if we want to change our direction, we need to take time to focus and meditate on what God is saying.

I have been working on my love walk. I was hard and had no concept of sonship, so I could not pass that onto my own sons. God wanted to teach me, so he used my oldest son, Shannon, to help me learn this lesson and pass it on to my children.

Shannon had saved up to go to a Youth With A Mission (YWAM) discipleship training outreach. He had worked hard and saved half the money required: about $1,500. I was going to supply the other half. Through a foolish action, Shannon put himself in a position that all his money got stolen. I was furious and told him that it was too bad: your fault; you pay.

God had a different idea. He talked to me that night and said, "I want him to go, and you are going to send him." A couple of days later, I lost my job, but I was determined to obey God. In the end, that minor setback of losing my job actually allowed me to make double that year. In fact, I was on a new job in two days and never even missed a paycheck.

My sending Shannon to YWAM, despite his blowing it, demonstrated to him the mercies of God. It showed him that God was his father and, thus, that he had an inheritance. Sons and daughters have inheritances; hirelings work for wages. His mission trip would eventually change him and me.

Joseph is the perfect example of a word, patiently received, changing a man. God "sent a man before them, even Joseph… whose feet they hurt with fetters: he was laid in iron [literally, his soul came into the iron]: Until the time that his word came: the word of the Lord tried him" (Ps. 105:17-19). Joseph was the favorite son of his father, Jacob. When Joseph was just a young man, God gave him a dream about his destiny to be the head of Jacob's clan. His brothers hated him for his arrogance and sold him into slavery, effectively killing his destiny, or so they thought. Joseph descended through slavery and ended up as a slave in prison in Egypt. This ended his destiny, or so he thought, "but God was with him" (Acts 7:9). Then Pharaoh, the ruler of Egypt, had a dream, and through God's sovereignty, Joseph was in a place to interpret that dream.

Pharaoh elevated Joseph to Prime Minister, and he was ruling Egypt when his brothers came looking for food.

God could have left Joseph at home, pampered and favored, and given him the interpretation for Pharaoh's dream. Then when he was 30, God could have sent him down to Egypt on the day Pharaoh dreamt his dream. Joseph would have had the strategies for overcoming the famine and Pharaoh would have made him Prime Minister, just as he did, and all Israel would have been saved. But Joseph would not have been changed from the arrogant, self-centered, insensitive egotist that he was. *God is not interested in just getting a job done; He wants sons and daughters whom He can train to rule and reign with Him.* To claim that destiny, we must go through His schooling and learn to patiently trust His word. The word is a two-edged sword, designed not only to cut through all the outer circumstance and resistance to it, but also to cut through our inner realities and resistance to it.

It took 15 years for the promise in the dream (of all his family bowing before him) to come to pass. Joseph went through that downward path of rejection by his brothers, to slavery in a foreign land, to a prison. The iron chains, the Scriptures say, enter his soul. That means the restrictions got right into his emotions. He lost all the ability to use any of his own influence or power to free himself. The last straw came when Joseph pleaded with Pharaoh's butler (cupbearer) to "make mention of me unto Pharaoh, and bring me out of this house" (Gen. 40:14). Yet the chief butler "forgot him" (Gen. 40:23 NKJV). At the end of two full years, "Pharaoh dreamed" (Gen. 41:1).

Two years! I think Joseph had probably given up hope for salvation from the butler. He seemed doomed, but God made him "prosperous" (Gen. 39:2) even in the middle of his downward spiral. He was successful at everything he touched, but that success didn't bring him closer to the throne. It was the downward spiral that brought him into prison and put him next to a man who was close to Joseph's next boss. By that time, the tribulation that Joseph went through had developed patience in him. He had experienced God's hand of protection even in persecution, and he was ready to hope only in God and thus was ready for promotion. His character had changed, and he could say to his brothers, "Fear not...am I in the place of God? ...[You] thought evil against me; but God meant it [for] good" (Gen. 50:19-20). God both saved Israel and perfected Joseph.

This is the message: God turns evil into good if we will let Him. Resting in Him is the only way. Situations may look bad for us but "though our outward man perish, yet the inward man is renewed day by day. For our light affliction, which is but for a moment [in light of eternity], worketh for us a far more exceeding and eternal weight of glory" (2 Cor. 4:16-17). Many Scriptures testify to this truth. Job said, "When He hath tried me, I shall come forth as gold" (Job 23:10), and James says, "The trying of your faith worketh patience...that ye may be perfect and entire, wanting nothing" (James 1:3-4).

God wants to give us that word and bless us. He doesn't want us to earn it but rather to receive it as an inheritance. The problem is that often children who receive an inheritance before they have the ability to manage it are destroyed by what should be a good gift. God doesn't want that to happen, so He prepares us in our hearts to be able to manage our inheritance. Can we wait until the Father's time, until He says we are ready? If we can, then we can cease from our own labors in trying to bring it to pass and enter His rest. "He that [has] entered into His rest, he also [has] ceased from his own works [labor]" (Heb. 4:10).

The children of Israel were promised a different type of existence in the land they were to receive than the land they had left. Their provision was to come from a different source. They used to grow their food through irrigation by using treadmills to pump the water onto the land. God said that this land was different and that they would no longer water it with their foot (labor). Instead, it would drinks the rain of heaven (see Deut. 11:10-11). God was moving them into rest, from labor into receiving, from a position as a hireling to a new position as a son. Along with this new status also came a new method of discipline to help them walk in God's way: no rain!

No longer could they depend on their own efforts to provide; they now had to depend on God. In our nature this presents a problem: what happens if God doesn't come through? Worry is actually our faith that satan will have his way because we see the impossible circumstance, rather than believing that God's word will prevail. Israel could no longer make things happen; they had to wait on God. We also must learn to wait on God. The Word says, "A man's gift makes room for him, and brings him before great men" (Prov. 18:16 NKJV).

Can we wait for Him? Can we "be anxious for nothing" and "commit [our] way to the Lord, trust also in Him, and He shall bring it to pass" (Phil. 4:6; Ps. 37:5 NKJV)? It is good to wait patiently for the Lord (see Lam. 3:25-26). Our patience in waiting allows our fruit (our character) to develop so that God can produce a harvest. We will even need patience in Heaven. "How long, O Lord.... It was said…that they should rest yet for a little season, until…" (Rev. 6:10-11).

I am still working on this aspect of my character. Recently I activated my company for about six months, hired 14 men, and did about $300,000 worth of work. I did it because a door opened. However, I never waited for confirmation or for a word. I just jumped in. The fruit of all this effort (getting back on the treadmill) was a big zero; I broke even. I was in too big a hurry to catch an opportunity and couldn't rest.

God is never in a hurry. There is never a portrayal of God running except when the Father ran to meet the prodigal; otherwise God's plan unfolds at what would seem an intolerably slow and steady pace. The truth is, the pace is always quickening, as events tie together. "The Lord is not slack concerning His promise, as some men count slackness; but is longsuffering.... But the day of the Lord will come as a thief in the night" (2 Pet. 3:9-10). With the natural mind we often don't comprehend the answers to our prayers until "suddenly" it appears. "The Lord…shall suddenly come to His temple" (Mal. 3:1).

So we have to learn to wait for all the pieces of the puzzle to fall into place. We are told that He is a shelter in the time of storm. To get the benefit of resting in His shadow, we must stop moving. "I sat down under his shadow with great delight" (Song of Sol. 2:3). You can't get the benefit of shade by running through it.

Things take time. Every great harvest starts with seeds; every great ministry starts as ministry to those God has placed around you, in your own home. You must be a partaker of the truth yourself before you offer it to others. "The husbandman that [is laboring] must be first partaker of the fruits" (2 Tim. 2:6).

Are you looking for a ministry or an answer for prayer? Let God work it out in you first. Prove it in your own life. Wait until it is life for you and not just doctrine before you take it to someone else, "For if a man does not know how to rule his own house, how will he take care of the church of God?" (1 Tim. 3:5 NKJV).

David learned to deal with a lion and a bear in the context of his job as a shepherd before he dealt with Goliath. Thus David could reassure Saul that he could handle the situation. "Thy servant kept his father's sheep, and...slew both the lion and the bear: and this uncircumcised Philistine shall be as one of them" (1 Sam. 17:34,36). David didn't just suddenly appear as the savior; he had been in training for years.

God has His "suddenlies," but we must learn to wait in the place He puts us and be fruitful there. We will not witness in China if we cannot witness to our neighbors, friends, and coworkers here. The location or situation will not change who we are and how much we depend on God's leading and empowering. We must be changed, not our situations.

Do we have worries and cares? "[Cast] all your care upon Him, for He cares for you" (1 Pet. 5:7 NKJV). "Be anxious for nothing. ...Commit your way to the Lord...and He shall bring it to pass. If we have ceased from our own labors then...the servant of the Lord must not strive" to try to make things happen (see Phil. 4:6 NKJV; Ps. 37:5; Heb. 4:10; 2 Tim. 2:24). Our efforts to "help God" or "hurry God" will result in an Ishmael.

Ishmael was Abram's son, the result of Abram's trying to make God's word happen. Sarah was God's chosen vessel to conceive the child of promise, but when it didn't look like that was going to happen, Sarah devised a scheme whereby she would bear children through her maid Hagar. Even though the plan produced a son, it didn't produce an heir or the desired result, which was the fulfillment of God's purpose.

When Isaac was born, Ishmael taunted and teased him. Isaac was the product of Abraham's faith; Ishmael was the product of his flesh. The flesh always fights the Spirit. "We...as Isaac...are the children of promise. But as then he [Ishmael] that was born after the flesh [striving] persecuted him that was born after the Spirit, even so it is now" (Gal. 4:28-29).

Evil is not the only enemy of the best; good is also the enemy of the best. The fruit of the tree of the knowledge of good and evil appeared "good...pleasant...to be desired" (Gen. 3:6), but it brought death. Charging into what appears good indicates what is in our hearts. Anytime we wait for God, no matter what the panic, it is a test to see if we are in charge or if God is in charge. If we "have to do something," our accusation against God is, "You don't care as much as I do," or "You don't understand the situation as well as I do."

Saul panicked when Samuel did not appear on the day the Lord had appointed. Saul said, "I forced myself therefore, and offered a burnt offering" (1 Sam. 13:12). He had to go against his own conscience because Samuel appeared to be late. As is usual, the answer from God (Samuel in this case) showed up minutes after the disobedience had taken place. Had Saul waited another half hour, he would not have lost the kingdom. It wasn't the sin—the event—that caused the loss of the kingdom; it was the heart not being right. The event just exposed it.

God is in the business of exposing hearts, not to rebuke us, but rather so we will repent and not trust ourselves. Unless we see our condition, we will, like Saul, attempt to shift the blame (see 1 Sam. 13:11-12). If we can wait patiently, and not just want the circumstances changed, then we can still rejoice when tribulation comes. "But we glory in tribulations…knowing that tribulations [works]: and patience, experience; and experience, hope: And hope [makes] not ashamed" (Rom. 5:3-5) if our hope is in Jesus and our dwelling with Him. If our hope is in how well we do and how things appear, then when tribulation comes, it will only bring pain.

Jeanne and I have learned not to panic while we wait. As mentioned in an the previous chapter, we once waited three months for God to arrange circumstances with a house that He had promised was ours. The house was beyond our price range, and the owners were stuck on their price. There seemed no way in the natural that we would ever get this place. The house had a huge atrium attached to the back. The problem with the atrium was that it had a gravel floor, and with the water table in the area so high, it smelled like a root cellar. The roof of the atrium was just corrugated fiberglass panels, and the rain came in, adding to the musty smell. The temperatures in the house would climb to over 100 degrees because of the atrium. The humidity stayed at 100 percent because the house had to be locked up and could not be vented. When people opened the front door they would be blasted with the heat, the humidity, and the smell. That was enough to convince most people that the atrium had to be torn down, which would cost thousands of dollars. For me, I saw the potential; others only saw the problem. God used this situation to keep the house on the market. The owners had moved to Vancouver and got frustrated with the lack of activity on their house. They switched listing agents and got one who convinced them to dump the property. Jeanne and I just needed to give it a rest and let God motivate the sellers to sell. We didn't have to bargain or fight, but just wait and trust the word that the house was ours.

This is why patience and rest bring peace. Jesus said, "Peace I leave with you, My peace I give to you; not as the world gives…. Let not your heart be troubled, neither let it be afraid" (John 14:27 NKJV). In the world, an absence of war constitutes a state of peace. In God's economy, peace is given right in the midst of war. Jesus had already said that He had not come to bring peace (cessation of war) but rather a sword. In the midst of this division, by trusting in Him, we can have a state of calm.

One of Jesus' earliest pre-incarnation appearances was as Melchizedek, King of Salem.[3] Hebrews 7:2 gives us the interpretation of his titles, which are used to denote his characteristics, as King of Righteousness and King of Peace. If Jesus is to be the King of Peace, then His subjects must live in the land of peace.

The peace of God is a weapon; we are to wear it as part of our armor. "And your feet shod with the preparation of the gospel of peace" (Eph. 6:15). It is interesting that we don't just put on the Gospel (good news) of peace, but that we put on the preparation also. We must settle some things in our hearts if we are to walk in peace. Peace was to go on our feet, which indicates our walk: the way we live, work, engage in relationships, counsel, etc. But there is a preparation, a posturing, that is required, enabling us to come into that peace. It is an ongoing revelation, because at each level of demonic attack, there will be a new level of defensive and offensive armor required.

Jesus said to His disciples, "When they bring you to...magistrates and authorities, do not worry about how or what you should answer, or what you should say. For the Holy Spirit will teach you...what you ought to say" (Luke 12:11-12 NKJV). God is saying, "Determine in your heart before the battle to leave it in My hand." No sword fighting in our minds or planning will be allowed, for these take away from our peace. We (our spirit man) must speak to our souls on how to act because our spirit is in tune with the Holy Spirit and knows the outcome of every situation.

David realized this counseling within his soul caused him grief. "How long shall I take counsel in my soul, having sorrow in my heart daily? How long shall [my] enemy be exalted over me?" (Ps. 13:2). He had to learn to speak to his soul. "Why are you cast down, O my soul? And why are you disquieted within me? Hope in God, for I shall yet praise Him" (Ps. 42:5 NKJV). Finally he could say, "Return unto thy rest, O my soul; for the Lord hath dealt bountifully with thee" (Ps. 116:7).

As we said earlier, for every promise, there is a testing in the form of a wilderness that is usually just the opposite of the provision. The promises we make in a time of peace, God always extracts in a time of war. One thing about war in the world is that the plans that are made have to be scrapped as soon as the enemy is encountered. The confusion, smoke, fear, noise, interference, and unexpected responses that the enemy exhibits usually cause us to throw all of our plans out the window. When we plan for what we think will happen, it seldom works out that way. With God, because He does know what the enemy has up his sleeve, planning for what we think might happen only limits what we allow Him to do.

In the desert the children of Israel were always in a panic. They were like a skittish horse, afraid of their own shadow. They were always expecting the worst, so whenever a problem arose, their common reaction was to grumble and complain. They were never able to exhibit any form of patience. Even though they had seen God come through time after time, they were never able to rest in His good plan for them. This was rebellion, and it was manifested in their constant desire to turn back. "They turned back and tempted God, and *limited* the Holy One of Israel" (Ps. 78:41). The word translated "limit" had the root *tâvâh*—meaning, scratching a mark.[4] They basically drew a line in the sand and said, "This far and no farther." Their words created a literal line of resistance. Israel's constant voicing of their fears, through complaints, actually prevented

God from using them at all. If they had trusted God as Joshua and Caleb did, they could have patiently waited for God to use the difficult circumstance for their benefit.

This attitude of not trusting God to have a good plan was demonstrated right at the beginning of their journey. God had told Moses that Pharaoh would not let the people go, but that when He was done with him, he would not only let them go but that "you shall plunder the Egyptians" (Exod. 3:22 NKJV). Pharaoh responded to the initial request by increasing the workload, and the leader of the people cried, "You made us…detested by Pharaoh and…have put a sword in their hand to slay us" (Exod. 5:21 AMP). If they had trusted that God was going to fight their battle, they could have said, "Let's sit back and watch how God is going to fix this."

Habakkuk learned the secret of waiting. He had prophetically seen Babylon invading Israel and had protested to God. After pouring out his complaints to God, he knew he was just whining and that God would straighten out his thinking. "I will…watch to see what He will say…and what I shall answer when I am reproved" (Hab. 2:1). This attitude allowed him to express a trustful attitude when everything was going wrong. He later could make this faith statement:

> *Although the fig tree shall not blossom, neither shall fruit be in the vines; the labor of the olive shall fail, and the fields shall yield no meat; the flock shall be cut off from the fold, and there shall be no herd in the stalls: Yet I will rejoice in the Lord…. [He] is my strength, and He will make…me to walk upon…high places (Habakkuk 3:17-19).*

161

Habakkuk saw the storm coming but recognized that the enemy was being sent (or allowed) by God (see Hab. 1:12). God was using a hard situation to correct Israel, as a Father would do. God always has our good at heart. "Whom the Lord loves He chastens, and scourges every son whom He receives" (Heb. 12:6 NKJV). If you are not chastised, you are not sons (see Heb. 12:8). "He [chastens us] for our profit that we might be partakers of His holiness. Now no chastening for the present [seems] to be joyous, but grievous: nevertheless afterward it [yields] the peaceable fruit of righteousness...lift up the hands which hang down" (Heb. 12:10-12).

What is the writer trying to say? Don't look at the hard things as bad, but rather see them as God's method to, through patience, move us through righteousness into His holiness. The storms are coming, but God is the Master of the storms. It doesn't matter who is conducting the storms; God is the author, the composer, and not even satan can stray from the score written. God will not leave you (in satan's hands) nor forsake you. Just as God had an ark prepared for Noah's deliverance, so He has one for us.

Boats are designed to ride out storms, and we all try to get a big one that we feel safe in. The problem is not when the boat gets in the storm. The problem is when the storm gets in the boat. We need to stay in peace so that God has the liberty to do whatever it takes to save us. There is a storm coming that no boat will be able to ride out. The only safe place will be walking on the water, walking in peace with Jesus. So don't panic when your boat starts to sink. Jesus rebuked His disciples because they panicked when their boat was sinking. "How is it that you have no faith" (Mark 4:40 NKJV). We need to have the worldview that the Kingdom is not affected by the situations it comes up against. It is the presence of the King that causes those situations to align to His purposes. Knowing this allows us to set out and patiently run the race that is set before us (see Heb. 12:1).

Even though God wants us to patiently endure, He also wants us to call out to Him. Jesus understood and responded, "In the days of His flesh,…[He] offered up prayers and supplications with strong crying and tears" (Heb. 5:7). He pushed on God, and God encourages us to do the same thing. "Call unto Me, and I will answer [you]" (Jer. 33:3). Jesus encouraged His disciples to be persistent in prayer: "Shall not God avenge His own elect, which cry day and night unto Him, though He bear long with them? I tell you that He will avenge them speedily" (Luke 18:7-8).

Even in Heaven, the martyrs knew how God wanted them to respond, "They cried with a loud voice, saying, How long, O Lord…avenge our blood…it was said unto them…rest yet for a little season, until their…brethren… should be killed" (Rev. 6:10-11). They're crying out for justice, but God says that more must be killed first! Do we see that God's ways are not ours, but that He wants us to call for Him to move? Why? It's our realm; He has limited Himself not to move unless we ask Him to. Our crying out is not an indication of fear but rather of reliance. He needs to intervene or we are lost, but we know that if we invite Him into the situation, He will fix it.

Jesus' own mother got a rebuke for trying to get Him to fix an embarrassing situation at the marriage in Galilee. But guess what? She got what she asked for. She knew that He would respond, and even after the rebuke, she told the servants to respond to what He would say. She demonstrated patient expectation (see John 2:3-11).

Jeanne persisted in prayer for her own mother. Jeanne had been praying for months for her mother and felt God was going to do something on a particular day. She prayed for an hour while traveling to visit her mother and then for another hour while she was waiting for her to come home. Jeanne's sister had gone to the doctor with a swollen gland on her neck. Because of the long period of prayer, Jeanne's faith was elevated, and when her mother and sister arrived home, she asked her sister if she could pray for the very large lump on her neck. As Jeanne prayed, the lump, which was the size of a grapefruit, seemed to jiggle and decrease. Her sister felt it and ran to look in the mirror. Jeanne prayed several times more, and each time the mass decreased until it was not even noticeable. Her sister had been planning a trip but because of the lump had been debating whether or not to go. After the prayer she decided that she was healed enough to go. Later they found out that she was diagnosed with mononucleosis and should have been extremely sick and weak, but instead she enjoyed a nice holiday. This demonstration of power was the catalyst for Jeanne's mother's salvation just days later.

We need to push until God manifests His authority in our realms. Jesus said, "The kingdom of heaven suffers violence, and the violent take it by force" (Matt. 11:12 NKJV). Now pushing and demanding and constantly asking may not seem like exhibiting patience and resting, but God says it is. "Ask and keep on asking...seek and keep on seeking...knock and keep on knocking" (Luke 11:9 AMP). Jesus is challenging them to patiently persist, not being put off by the first "no." Earlier He had expressed this in a parable about a man asking a friend for some bread late at night: "Although he will not get up and supply him anything because he is his friend, yet because of his shameless persistence and insistence he will get up and give him as much as he needs" (Luke 11:8 AMP).

As mentioned in a previous chapter, Bob Jones once talked to my wife and me concerning a situation with our son. He said that we must keep pushing back the territory that the devil had occupied. In addition to his analogy of slowly pushing the glass, he also related to us the story about his own battle contending with the devil for his father's salvation. God showed Bob that he was like a bulldog that had latched onto satan's little finger and that he could not shake off. This picture assured Bob that he could continue to aggressively demand the release of his father and be assured of his salvation. God does not make people change, but He does know whether they will or won't, and He may show us so that we can, through prayer, enter into what He is doing. Finally after several weeks of constant harassment from Bob, satan told Bob that he would let him have his request for his father (satan would release his grip on Bob's father), if Bob would let go. Bob came back, knowing now that he had the victory, saying, "No deal. I have cousins too."

Bob was telling us to push the advantage when we know God's will and to use patient persistence. Rest is not an attitude of relaxing, doing nothing. Rest is a ceasing from your own labors and worries and trusting in God's word concerning a situation.

The first year that I took time off from working was exciting. I knew God wanted to stretch me to trust Him. I was learning to rest. That didn't mean I didn't work; it just meant that I left the details in God's hands. It was fun. There was a heavy snowfall that winter, and the boys and I shoveled snow off of roofs to prevent their collapse. We made over $8,000 dollars and enjoyed each other's company. Then someone contacted me concerning doing a small contract for one weekend. That contract netted over $10,000. The blessings kept flowing, and by the time I went back to work nine months later, we had more money in the bank than when I stopped work.

Jeanne has been pushing and declaring health into her own body lately. She has seen both her thyroid medication and her eyeglass prescription reduced. Pushing is work, but it is not toil, and it is not striving; it is restfully exercising faith and authority.

The children of Israel were to enter into a rest in the land. This required them to push out the enemy, but it was not actually their job to win the war. It was only their job to show up for the battle, recognizing that God was going to fight for them. They did not possess the land "by their own sword, neither did their own arm save them: but Thy right hand, and Thine arm, and the light of Thy countenance, because Thou [had] favor unto them" (Ps. 44:3). "He [God] cast out the heathen...before them" (Ps. 78:55). Even nature was conspiring against the Canaanites. "The land is defiled...I do visit the iniquity thereof upon it, and the land itself [will vomit] out her inhabitants" (Lev. 18:25).

Rest is the ability to not sweat those things that are in God's realm. The expulsion of the Amorites was part of the initial covenant that God made with Abraham concerning the land. He had told Abraham, "But in the fourth generation they shall come [here] again, for the iniquity of the Amorites is not yet full" (Gen. 15:16). Rest is a posture for war. It lets the enemy know that his demise, in our opinion, is a done deal. It shows our lack of fear concerning his lies. We know the promise that God has given us and the victory that He won at the cross. Satan cannot prevent us from coming into the promise; only we can do that.

Hebrews speaks of the attitude of the early church:

> [You] *endured a great fight of afflictions...*[you] *were made a gazingstock both by reproaches and afflictions... and took joyfully the spoiling of your goods.... Cast not away therefore your confidence, which hath great recompense of reward. For ye have need of patience, that, after ye have done the will of God, ye might receive the promise* (Hebrews 10:32-36).

They could do this because they believed in the recompense and the promise. If we are not sure that God is in control, then we will panic and do something that is not in our realm of authority. Saul's inability to wait till Samuel showed up, as they had agreed, exposed his fears that God wasn't in control. "When I saw that the people were scattered from me, and that you did not come in the days appointed, and that the Philistines gathered together,...I felt compelled and offered a burnt offering" (1 Sam. 13:11-12 NKJV). That was not the king's job. So Samuel said to Saul, "You have done foolishly.... The Lord would have established your kingdom over Israel forever, but now your kingdom shall not continue..." (1 Sam. 13:13-14 NKJV). Seems like a harsh judgment, but Saul's actions were just an indication of the condition of his heart: "The Lord has sought for Himself a man after His own heart...because you have not kept what the Lord commanded you" (1 Sam. 13:14 NKJV).

Even Abraham, who had great patience, tried to "help" God and produced Ishmael. This error in judgment has caused trouble for the children of promise (Israel) ever since, "He that was born after the flesh persecuted him that was born after the Spirit; even so it is now" (Gal. 4:29). Anytime we take the initiative before God has birthed the promise, what is produced will become a burden at the least, or an enemy at the worst. We must have patience. Our posture of rest can be in response to a word from God.

Our kids had lots of problems in their teens, partially because we were ignorant of how much our position in the battle affected them. Jeanne had a word that "great shall be the peace of your children" (Isa. 54:13 NKJV). That word allowed us to rest, even when it seemed like hell itself was attacking our home. God was teaching us to have patience when the situations would say different. Our lack of patience is usually connected with our situations not changing or with other people not acting the way we think they should.

God isn't worried about situations and other people. He is always concerned about us and our thoughts and actions. If we will deal with ourselves, the other situations will look after themselves. "Bringing into captivity every thought to the obedience of Christ; and having in a readiness to revenge all disobedience, when your obedience is fulfilled" (2 Cor. 10:5-6). The order is always: first us, then those who trouble us. If we won't deal with our own thoughts, which reveal our hearts, then God won't change our situations. Those situations are the very things that cause us to react and reveal our hearts. They are necessary for us to recognize how evil we are. This all takes time and requires patience.

The greater our call, the longer will be our refining time. Paul went through a continual refining until he could say, "The signs of an apostle were wrought among you in all patience, in signs, and wonders, and mighty deeds" (2 Cor. 12:12). Paul stated that one of the signs of being an apostle was to operate with patience. He had previously laid out what he had to endure to get to where he was. He lists them as:

> *In labors…in stripes…in prisons…in deaths… five times received I* [39 lashes]. *Thrice was I beaten…, once was I stoned, thrice I suffered shipwreck* [24 hours once floating]*…; in journeyings often, in perils of waters, in perils of robbers, in perils by mine own countrymen, in perils by the heathen, in perils in the city, in perils in the wilderness, in perils in the sea, in perils among false brethren; in weariness and painfulness, in watchings often, in hunger and thirst, in fastings often, in cold and nakedness. Beside*

those things..., the care of all the churches [he kept the best till last]*"* (2 Corinthians 11:23-28).

It takes patience to endure. We are in a race, and we must run to finish. "Let us lay aside every weight [unnecessary care], and...sin [those things that will trip us up]..., and let us run with patience the race that is set before *us* [our own individual course], looking unto Jesus...who... endured...lest [you] be wearied and faint in your minds [literally, *soul*]" (Heb. 12:1-3). This race may not be a sprint; rather it may be a marathon; but it is your race. We are told to look at our captain (Jesus) as we run, not at all the other racers. They may be running a different race. If a marathon runner and a sprinter start at the same time, the marathon runner will appear to be losing; however, there is no comparison as both are running a different race.

The important thing is to endure and finish. Paul emphasizes this: "I have fought a good fight, I have finished my course [race], I have kept the faith...there is laid up for me a crown [wreath]" (2 Tim. 4:7-8). Why the victor's crown? He finished his race. We should adopt a patient attitude in this race because "Jesus [is] the author [originator] and finisher of our faith" (Heb. 12:2). He institutes the race and finishes it for us, if we remain faithful and endure. Jesus encouraged us to endure. "You will be hated by all for My name's sake. But he who endures to the end will be saved" (Matt. 10:22 NKJV). God is asking us to trust Him.

"Cast not away...your confidence, which hath great recompense of reward. For [you] have need of patience, that, after [you] have done the will of God, [you] might receive the promise....

Now the just shall live by faith: but if any man draw back, my soul shall have no pleasure in him" (Heb. 10:35-36, 38). Don't quit. God has spoken a word of faith to you: faith is always now, maybe just not yet. Promises come in seed form; the manifestation may need cultivation and watering, but if you will endure, it will come to fruit. The strength to endure comes from Jesus, but we must be willing to wait. "They that wait upon the Lord shall renew their strength...they shall run, and not be weary...walk, and not faint" (Isa. 40:31).

Our state of rest can be recognized by how much peace we have. When the car breaks down, when the fridge conks out, when the hot water tank starts leaking, can you hold your peace—especially when all of this occurs on the same day? The ability to rule over our own spirits is considered power by God. "He who rules his [own] spirit [is greater] than he who takes a city" (Prov. 16:32 NKJV). A constant unrest should alert us to areas of the flesh that are manifesting.

Wickedness is always stirring things up and agitating people; they never have any rest or peace (see Isa. 48:22). People with a restless spirit, who can't sit still and just meditate on God, who always have to be moving, will stir up dirt and mire eventually. A lack of peace indicates the presence of the wicked one. "The wicked are like the troubled sea, when it cannot rest, whose waters cast up mire and dirt. There is no peace, [says] my God, to the wicked" (Isa. 57:20-21). God uses the weapon of peace to defeat wickedness. "The God of peace shall bruise Satan under your feet shortly" (Rom. 16:20). The unrest in our souls and spirits is often an indication that we are chaffing under uncomfortable authority.

Power and authority come when we are positioned under authority, but an inability to stay under that authority indicates a rebellious area in our hearts. Therefore peace must be our umpire or arbitrator when we need to make a decision to obey. "Let the peace of God rule [arbitrate] in your hearts" (Col. 3:15). "And let the peace (soul harmony which comes) from Christ rule (act as umpire continually) in your hearts [deciding and settling with finality all questions that arise in your minds, in that peaceful state] to which...you were also called" (Col. 3:15 AMP).

Peace will dictate the choices you make. The flesh is always excited (stirred up) when something seems too good to be true. I have found that the more excited I got and the better something seemed, the more certain it was to be the flesh. God says that wars, tumult, and battles come from lusts, wars, tumults, and battles within us (see James 4:1). *Lust is a desire to get. Love is a desire to give.* The existence of restlessness, or wars, tumults, and battles (stirring up dirt and mire), indicates lusts within us that eventually surface and will cause envying and strife among us. It is always a desire of the flesh to get rather than give. The world says get and you will have more. God says give (sow) and you will reap a harvest and have more. This takes faith and faith based on understanding the Word. "My people are destroyed for lack of knowledge" (Hos. 4:6).

Lack of trust—demonstrated by the inability to wait for God to show up—cost Saul the kingdom. He lost his authority by not resting in the word spoken to him. He presumed he could react to the situation and do what was, in his opinion, necessary. The agitation in his own spirit should have twigged in his mind that he had stepped out of the spirit and into the presumption of the flesh. Presumption is a sin. Presumption is pride. Its various meanings are: bold to the excess, proceeding from excess of confidence, arrogant, insolent, willful or rash.[5] When we presume without asking, we are really saying, "I don't have to ask; I can do what I want. I don't need permission." At that point we step into the flesh because we are now out to *get* (which is lust).

When the children of Israel refused to go into the land, they were told of the consequences (40 years in the wilderness). At that point, they decided to change their minds and go in, but it was too late. They went up anyway; "...they presumed to go up...nevertheless the ark...of the Lord...departed not out of the camp. Then the Amalekites...smote them" (Num. 14:44-45). They presumed that they could change their minds and that God would repent, but the ark (the manifest presence of the Lord) didn't go with them, and they died. If their attitude had been the opposite, and they had truly repented, God might have found an intercessor to change His mind.

We need to step back into our spirit man and say, "Why am I doing this? Why am I reacting like this? Why don't I have peace?" When you feel compelled or forced to do something, it's not God. God has His seasons; we must be patient, relax, and wait for them.

> *For the vision is yet for an appointed time, but at the end it shall speak, and not lie: though it tarry, wait for it; because it will surely come, it will not tarry...his soul which*

173

is lifted up [proud, presumptuous] *is not upright in him:
but the just shall live by his faith* (Habakkuk 2:3-4).

ENDNOTES

1. Jim Eliot, *The Journals of Jim Elliot*, edited by Elisabeth Elliot (Grand Rapids, MI: Fleming H. Revell,
   1978), 174.

2. Spiros Zodhiates, *The Complete Word Study Old Testament* (Chattanooga, TN: AMG Publishers, 1992),
   #4762.

3. Hebrews 7:17 calls Jesus "….a priest forever according
   to the order of Melchizedek" (NKJV). We can know
   that Melchizedek was Christ because he was "without
   father, without mother, without genealogy, having neither beginning of days nor end of life, but made like
   the Son of God, he remains a priest perpetually"
   (Heb. 7:3 NASB). If the priesthood never changes,
   and if Christ is that priest, then He always was that
   priest.

4. Zodhiates, *The Complete Word Study Old Testament*
   (Chattanooga, TN: AMG Publishers, 1992), #8427,
   8428.

5. *Webster's New Twentieth Century Dictionary*, s.v.
   "Presumption."

Chapter 5

Catch Me, Daddy — Trust

God will trust us with His power if we can trust Him with our lives. What is trust? It's a confidence in the good qualities of another. That attitude is expressed by an accompanying action of reliance on that individual. Blondin, the French tightrope-walker of the 1800s, once asked his manager if he believed that he, The Great Blondin, could walk across Niagara Falls on a tight rope with a man on his back. His manager, Harry Colcord, insisted that he completely believed that Blondin could do it. Blondin replied. "If you trust me that much, come with me. I will carry you on my back." The proof of the statement "I trust you" was demonstrated in the fact that Harry did accompany him on his trek. He entrusted his life into Blondin's keeping.[1] That is what God is asking us to do.

Once I was asked to weld some lifting lugs on a large structural member so that it could be hoisted at a 70-degree angle. The piece weighed close to 140 tons and would require two cranes to set it in place. I called the company's engineering department, but they confessed their ignorance of where to locate the lugs to support the lift. I had no idea how to calculate the positions of the lugs, so I called up an engineering friend to see if he could help. Later that night, he called back with a negative answer, and I then knew what I had to do. I said to God, "You know how to do it. Please show me how." I was just going to bed and was pondering the problem when a formula popped into my mind. I jumped up and wrote it down before I forgot, and then I went to sleep.

The next day at work, I calculated out the lug positions according to the formula that God had given me and got them welded on. I was so excited about God speaking so specifically that I told everyone, including the superintendent, how I got the answer. He smiled and sarcastically remarked, "You know what will happen to you if you are wrong, don't you?"

My job was on the line, but I trusted God. If it worked, He got the glory; if it didn't, I got fired. It worked so well that I could have pushed that 140-ton piece with my little finger to line it up. It is exciting to trust God.

Jesus asks us all to do the same, to trust. He is not some con man, smiling with outstretched arms, saying, "Trust Me." This is the Creator of the universe, who has already laid His life down to redeem us, pleading, for our own sakes, to trust Him. Jesus asks us to become as little children in our attitude toward

Him. Children, with total trust toward their father, will often not even wait for their dad to turn around before they will leap and cry out, "Daddy, catch me." That is total trust in a loving father.

That trust response is the defining difference between those in the Kingdom and both the demonic realm and unregenerate man. "You believe that there is one God. You do well. Even the demons believe—and tremble" (James 2:19 NKJV). Though they know there is one God, they do not trust Him. They do not trust Him to do what is best for them. Satan suggested that God didn't want Adam and Eve to eat the fruit on the tree of the knowledge of good and evil because "God doth know that in the day ye eat...your eyes shall be opened; and ye shall be as gods" (Gen. 3:5). The lie that satan was propagating was that God didn't want them to be like Him, that He wanted to keep them in their place. This lie was also whispered to Job, "Shall mortal man be more just than God? ...He put no trust in His servants; and His angels He charged with folly: How much less in them that dwell in houses of clay [man]" (Job 4:17-19). This was an assault against God's character.

Satan even cast doubt on God's word being true: "[You] shall not surely die" (Gen. 3:4). With doubt about God's character and words ringing in their ears, Adam and Eve could no longer trust God but feared Him and broke relationship. Satan is using the same tactic today. When Jeanne was about to give birth to our first son, Shannon, the doctor said that she was going to require a Caesarean section. I had prayed and heard God say that it would be a normal birth. Jeanne believed what

God said and gave birth without the aid of a C-section. The doctors decided to pull the baby with forceps, which caused Shannon to convulse. They said he would have brain damage. We again refused to believe the doctors and claimed healing for our son. He turned out to be not only normal, but brilliant. God calls us to fight against negative words that assail us from all sides.

Since man received that first lie, God has been wooing man back into a marriage-like relationship, where there is mutual trust and love. He has kept His part and has remained faithful to His commitment, even when we have not. The fact that we have not, or could not, entrust ourselves to Him necessitated God's making all the moves required to re-establish that trust. He does this because He loves us and His main characteristic is love.

First Corinthians 13 is not just a description of the facets of love, but of God Himself, for God is love. Because God equals love, we can substitute one for the other. Here is my paraphrase: God suffers long, and God is kind. God is not envious. God does not brag and is not arrogant. God does not act unbecomingly, is not out for Himself, is not easily provoked, does not keep account of wrong suffered, and rejoices in truth. God bears all things, believes all things, hopes all things, endures all things. God never fails (see 1 Cor. 13:4-8).

Moses stated it elegantly: "God is not a man, that He should lie. ...Hath He said, and shall He not do it? Or hath He spoken, and shall He not make it good? ...He hath blessed; and I cannot reverse it" (Num. 23:19-20). God is not just as good as His word; He is His word. Psalm 138:2 (paraphrased) says that God "magnifies His word above His name." This is why Jesus is called the Word of God. That was the highest praise He could bestow because His word is His bond or covenant and is the direct expression of His integrity.

In another place Jesus said, "The words that I speak to you are spirit, and they are life" (John 6:63 NKJV). *To doubt what God has spoken is to doubt the very essence of God, His very nature.* If we can't trust Him, we will never do what He tells us to do and never experience His power. The disciples were given a challenge to "Go...saying, 'The kingdom of heaven is at hand.' Heal the sick, raise the dead, cleanse the lepers, cast out demons. Freely you received, freely give. Do not acquire gold, or silver...or a bag...or even two coats, or sandals...for the worker is worthy of his support" (Matt. 10:7-10 NASB). The disciples expressed a great deal of trust by going out strictly on the basis of His word. They were actually surprised when they discovered that His power was manifested in them and that demons actually were subject to them. If we are going to be Jesus' disciples, we will also have to demonstrate a level of trust.

Jeanne and I have learned to trust God even when it made no sense. When we moved to Lloydminster, we only had five months of work laid out before us, and yet we felt God wanted us to buy a house. That is trust, but it is also exciting because there is a sense that, when you go out on a limb with God, then you are in a place of power. That power comes from knowing secrets that no one else is aware of. It is a place of friendship.

God told Abraham what He was going to do because Abraham was His friend (see Gen. 18:17).

These places of trust become landmarks that we can look back on and encourage our souls with by remembering what God did. The patriarchs built altars and monuments as witnesses to what transpired in those places. Jesus likewise reminded the disciples of God's faithfulness in supplying their needs when He had sent them out with no supplies of their own. He reminded them to strengthen their faith just before He was to be betrayed. Trust is built by remembrance, and God expects us to remember what He has done so that He can get a return on His investment.

Hezekiah, the Bible says, "rendered not again according to the benefit done unto him; for his heart was lifted up: therefore there was wrath upon him, and upon Judah" (2 Chron. 32:25). Hezekiah did not respond properly because he chose to forget what God had done for him. We are told to "bless the Lord...and forget not all His benefits" (Ps. 103:2). Meditating on what God has done, bringing to remembrance the past benefits, allows us to trust God rather than looking and fearing our situations. *Our self-pity and self-centeredness dissolve in His presence.*

Even with all the disasters and personal persecution that assailed him, Jeremiah could say, "This I recall to my mind, therefore I have hope. ...His compassions fail not. They are new every morning" (Lam. 3:21-23). As Jeremiah meditated on God, he could prophesy a successful future to a people going into captivity and even set a date for a miraculous delivery from that captivity. He trusted God, and his trust aided the generations of people who walked with Daniel and Ezra and Nehemiah to do the same.

Ezra was "ashamed to [ask the king for] a band of soldiers...to help [protect] us against the enemy...because we had spoken unto the king, saying, The hand of our God is upon all them for good that seek Him" (Ezra 8:22). Trust requires an appropriate action to be real trust, and that will always engender a response from God. Remember what happened in Ezra's situation? "So we fasted and entreated our God for this, and He answered our prayer" (Ezra 8:23 NKJV).

Jeanne used to be so fearful that she didn't like going out into our yard in case a neighbor would see her and want to talk to her. God would give her assignments that would stretch her and built her trust in Him. He sent her to a lovely Catholic neighbor, whose name she didn't even know, with a word that God loved her. Jesus desired to draw her into a personal relationship with Him. Jeanne told her that she didn't need a mediator between her and God. The lady laughed and replied that this was the third time someone had said the very same thing to her that very week. Experiences like that build our trust levels and prepare us for more exciting assignments.

Our actions must match up with our words. When we make a declaration of trust, that God is going to accomplish something He has promised, we are declaring war on the kingdom of darkness. We are in essence declaring that the Kingdom of God is going to bring the light in and throw back the darkness. Both God and satan are interested in testing our commitment, which is really our trust, and bring pressure to bear. God is trying to change us. Satan is trying to change the situation and nullify the word. If we are not in the center of God's will in a matter but are tentative or sitting on the fence, it is like dwelling along a border. In a war, the battles are fought along the border and an advance by either army will cross that border and run us over. The worst place a Christian can be is at the edge of a commitment. Be hot or cold God commands, but not lukewarm (see Rev. 3:15-16).

One of the best indicators of our commitment is the speed with which we respond to things we don't understand. *Slow obedience is disobedience.* For example, once when the kids were small, Jeanne was praying and God impressed her that something was wrong and she should go downstairs. She immediately went down, only to find the boys had wrapped some crepe paper around an exposed light bulb and it was just starting to smolder. A few minutes of hesitation on Jeanne's part would have spelled disaster in the form of a fire.

Abraham was quick to respond to the command to sacrifice Isaac. "Take...Isaac...and offer him.... And Abraham rose up early in the morning" (Gen. 22:2-3). His quick obedience resulted in blessing. "Because thou...hast not withheld thy son,... I will bless thee, and...I will multiply thy seed.... Thy seed shall possess the gates of his enemies" (Gen. 22:16-17). That blessing gave him power and authority over his enemies. The children of Israel, on the other hand, were a day slow in responding to God's command to take the land. "They rose up early in the morning...saying...we...will go up unto the place which the

Lord hath promised: for we have sinned. And Moses said...
Go not up, for the Lord is not among you...But they presumed to go up...and the Canaanites...smote them" (Num.
14:40-42,44-45).

The timing was the same, they both responded the next day,
but the heart's obedience came immediately with Abraham and
only came to the children of Israel after they had been told the
consequences of their rebellion. The timing in the heart was
what God judged, not the actions. The window of opportunity
had passed for the children of Israel, and they had no power or
authority on their own to conquer the land.

Our actions, when we are coming up against something we
fear, will indicate if we trust God or ourselves. If we trust ourselves, then we will be slow to obey. If it is God we trust, there
will be an excitement and an anticipation of what God is going
to do to solve the problem we are afraid of. This excitement will
enable us to quickly respond to His promptings. Though we
may not have the answer to the problem, we will have the trust.

Abraham quickly answered Isaac's question about where the
sacrifice was with a prophetic declaration of trust. "[Isaac]
said...Behold the fire and the wood: but where is the lamb...?
And Abraham said...God will provide Himself a lamb for a
burnt offering" (Gen. 22:7-8). Abraham believed that God
would solve this dilemma of how to sacrifice Isaac and yet have
him still be the vehicle through whom the blessing would flow.
Abraham trusted "that God was able to raise [Isaac]...from the
dead" (Heb. 11:19). This situation might look too hard, but in
Abraham's mind, it wasn't going to turn out badly. If we are

going to walk in the same authority in which Abraham walked, we must act like him and not look at the problem but rather see the answer. We are to stand on the promise, look past the problem, and see the provision, which Jesus will supply.

When everything fails, when all hope seems gone and the pressure is about to buckle our resolve, we get to see just where our trust is placed. God already knows. He is never disillusioned with us because He has no illusions about us. He knows our weaknesses, even if we don't. When we start to sink, we will grasp at any straw that we think will save us. "Some trust in chariots, and some in horses: but we will remember the name of the Lord our God" (Ps. 20:7).

Abraham called the name of the place where God provided a ram for the sacrifice instead of Isaac: *Jehovah-Jireh* (which means "the Lord will provide"). The place of seeming sacrifice is usually the place of provision. Can you trust God to do the same for you? If not, then that was just a good story that affected Abraham's stature with God, but not yours. *Trust* means putting yourself in a place where, if God doesn't come through, you are in trouble.

It is your creative words in agreement with God in your realm of authority that allows God's word to be manifested. God wants us to partner with Him in the creative process. Jeanne and I began one creative process when Jeanne had a dream about a house on some considerable acreage. In the dream she not only saw the house but the neighbor's houses as well. She could even describe the shapes, the colors, and the locations of the garages. The Spirit had given me a plan for a different type of house, so I drew it out and asked Jeanne if it looked like that. She got excited and said it was exactly as she had seen in the dream.

With this knowledge, we bought and started to build the house on our acreage. The only problem was that the houses across the road were not exactly as she had seen in the dream. However, within two years, one of the neighbors built a garage and the other changed the siding on their house to match the colors Jeanne had seen in the dream. God worked through us in that house and did many miraculous things. I did a Bible study with the guys that I hired to help me build the house and was able to lead one of the men into a personal relationship with Jesus.

If we can trust God, He can do awesome things for us. If you disavow or lose trust in His words, there is no creative power in them in your life. What God wants to accomplish with and through you is thwarted. Israel, in the wilderness, could never get on the same page as God because they never learned to trust. "Because they believed not in God, and trusted not in His salvation. ...They turned back...and limited the Holy One of Israel" (Ps. 78:22,41). As we discussed earlier, by their attitudes, the Israelites actually drew a line in the sand and told God, "We will not cross this line." They had reached the limit of their trust and were not willing to change.

Jesus experienced the same problem when He encountered unbelief and lack of trust in His hometown: "They were offended at Him. ...He did not do many mighty works there because of their unbelief" (Matt. 13:57-58 NKJV). This verse shows the importance of our relationship with Jesus and the complete necessity of the Church cooperating with God in order to manifest the Kingdom in the world. We have the responsibility, because only the Church, not the world, has the relationship to hear God's will and speak it into our realms of authority. Unless we can trust God and obey, in trust, what He says, the world will not escape from the judgment that they have brought upon themselves. We are the salt and the light. They need us or they will perish.

If we put hope in anything outside of God—education, government, good examples, religion, science, human nature, money, doctors, evolution, etc.—then these have become our gods. We will become immobilized, mute and deaf, if we trust in these. Their idols are:

> *The work of men's hands* [that]*...have mouths, but they speak not: eyes...but they see not...ears, but they hear not: noses...but they smell not...hands, but they handle not: feet...but they walk not: neither speak they.... They that make them are like unto them; so is every one that* **trusts** *in them. ...Ye that fear the Lord, trust in the Lord: He is their help and their shield* (Psalm 115:4-8,11).

Jeremiah goes further and says, "Cursed be the man that [trusts] in man.... Blessed is the man that [trusts] in the Lord, and whose hope [is in] the Lord" (Jer. 17:5,7). In my own life, I had to repent and break off the curse that came because I trusted in my own ability and work ethic to get me ahead in the business world. I am not saying that people should not work hard; I am saying that we should not trust in our ability to work hard.

Just a short time after I repented for trusting my own ability, I had a chance to minister this truth to a young hockey player. He had come for ministry because he was having trouble with his coach. (I didn't realize until later that he was a professional and played in the NHL.) He explained that he was not able to produce whenever he was put on the power play when the opposing team had a penalty. I got him to forgive his coach for his negative reactions and then to repent for trusting in himself, in his own abilities. Two nights later, he was playing in a televised game and was able to score two goals on the power play. He went on to have a personal best season even though his team did poorly.

We must be aware of the things we are placing our trust in. Some of the things we trust in are the very things God wants to deliver us from. "Because thou hast relied on the king of Syria, and not…on the Lord…therefore is the… king of Syria escaped out of thine hand" (2 Chron. 16:7). God had intended King Asa to have eventually removed the threat that Syria posed to Judah, but his lack of trust immobilized him and prevented God from carrying out his deliverance. God stated it in the next verse, "For the eyes of the Lord run to and fro throughout the whole earth, to show Himself strong in the behalf of them whose heart is perfect toward Him" (2 Chron. 16:9).

God was looking to establish Asa's authority in the region and bring peace, but Asa trusted in the wrong thing. As a result, "Thou [Asa] hast done foolishly: therefore from henceforth thou shalt have wars" (2 Chron. 16:9). Asa had on a previous occasion trusted God to defeat the Ethiopian army of over a million men. He had said, "Lord, it is nothing with Thee to help, whether with many, or with them that have no power: help us, O Lord our God; for we rest on Thee" (2 Chron. 14:11). That victory stirred up so much fear in the nations round about that Asa had 20 years of peace, even though "in those times there was no peace.... And nation was destroyed of nation...for God did vex them with all adversity" (2 Chron. 15:5-6). Trusting in God to fight for them brought peace. Fear, resulting in trusting men to fight for them, brought war. Asa's anger against the prophet who tried to rebuke him, and later other innocent people, was just a manifestation of that fear. Fear exposed the lack of trust and limited what God was able to do for Israel.

Our attitudes will always determine our altitude in God. Our attitudes come out of our heart.

Evil attitudes: "Those things which proceed out of the mouth come forth from the heart; and they defile the man. For out of the heart proceed evil thoughts, murders, adulteries, fornications, thefts, false witness, blasphemies" (Matt. 15:18-19).

Good attitudes: "But...good ground are they, which in an honest and good heart, having heard the word, keep it, and bring forth fruit with patience" (Luke 8:15).

If our heart is right, in trusting God, then we can leave our promotion in His hands: "Let another man praise thee and not thine own mouth..." (Prov. 27:2). We can also leave our desires in God's hands. "Where do wars and fights come from among you? Do they not come from your desires for pleasure that war

188

in your members? You lust and do not have. You murder and covet and cannot obtain. You fight and war. Yet you do not have because you do not ask" (James 4:1-2 NKJV).

We would rather strive on our own than trust God and ask, because we are not dead to our self-life. The Book of James says that we lust, and lust is always a desire to get while love is a desire to give. Trust allows God to give to you and to promote you. He has already put in you everything that you need to succeed. "A man's gift maketh room for him, and bringeth him before great men" (Prov. 18:16).

Jesus exemplified how we should trust God: "Let this mind be in you, which was also in Christ Jesus: Who...made Himself of no reputation, and took upon Him the form of a servant...He humbled Himself, and became obedient unto death" (Phil. 2:5-8). If we do that, then God can respond as He did with Jesus: "God also hath highly exalted Him" (Phil. 2:9).

Somebody once approached Jeanne to pray for them because they were going to preach somewhere at another assembly that coming Sunday. Jeanne also had to preach, and it was going to be her first time. She would have liked to have someone pray for *her*, but God told her that if she would pray for this man, that He would look after her. That night, after preaching, she gave an invitation for those who needed prayer. People responded and salvations, healings, and deliverances occurred. God always responds when we come to Him in trust.

Our level of trust in the faithfulness of God can easily be determined by how much we allow Him to promote us versus how much we promote ourselves. Even when we decide to let God be God in our lives, our heart attitude is revealed by our tendency to complain when things don't work out the way we were expecting:

> ...*I have learned, in whatsoever state I am, therewith to be content. I know both how to be abased, and I know how to abound: every where and in all things I am instructed both to be full and to be hungry, both to abound and to suffer need. I can do all things through Christ which strengtheneth me* (Philippians 4:11-13).

The children of Israel never changed their attitudes (hearts) as is witnessed by the fact that they never stopped grumbling and complaining. Of the ten tests alluded to in Numbers 14:22, murmuring and complaining were prominent in nine of them. Their lack of trust concerning His promise brought a judgment: "I have heard the murmurings of the children of Israel, which they murmur against Me. ...As truly as I live, saith the Lord, as ye have spoken in Mine ears, so I will do to you: your carcasses shall fall in this wilderness; and all...which have murmured against Me" (Num. 14:27-29).

Their default expression, in response to any hardship or seeming setback to receiving the promise, was, "Would God that we had died in the land of Egypt! or would God we had died in this wilderness" (Num. 14:2). They got exactly what was in their hearts to receive. Caleb, on the other hand, received a different promise: "because he had another spirit with him...I [God] will bring [him] into the land...and his seed shall possess it" (Num. 14:24). Attitude determines altitude. We must learn to see our hearts and pray, "You desire truth in the inward parts, and in the hidden part… make me to know wisdom" (Ps. 51:6 NKJV).

God is for us, but we must allow Him to change us to be able to prosper when He changes our circumstances. He has a hope and a future for us. He said "the meek shall inherit the earth" (Ps. 37:11), not the proud and boastful. We can judge the condition of our hearts by what comes out of our mouths.

God has put His thoughts in you to make them your thoughts. "The preparations of the heart in man, and the answer of the tongue, is from the Lord. …Commit thy works unto the Lord, and thy thoughts shall be established" (Prov. 16:1,3). God's desires for us are higher than our own. "Eye has not seen, nor ear heard, neither have entered into the heart of man, the things which God has prepared for those who love Him" (1 Cor. 2:9).

Lack of trust, which is fear, will keep us from claiming what is rightfully ours. Jeanne and I once were looking for a car that was easy on gas. We thought we would be better off if I had a little car to go to work in. However, we didn't ask God what car we should get; we assumed. We found a little Mini Morris and put a fleece out to the Lord. Fleeces are designed to confirm what you already know, but we were using this one as a source of direction. God was gracious and answered our test. We wanted to make sure the car was reliable and would start in the winter. We asked God to give us a sign that this was our car; it must start in the first ten tries. Ten tries! We used such a ridiculously high number, I am sure, just because we wanted that car.

It didn't start, however, until the 11th time. We bought it anyway! What a disaster that car turned out to be. I eventually gave it away for one dollar just because I was so sick of fixing it. Our fear of not getting a good car resulted in our buying a lemon. I was afraid that I would never have enough money to retire on. I was afraid I would never get a secure job. My fears drove me to try to make it myself. It took God a long time, and I had a lot of disasters, before I yielded to His ways.

Not everybody will come around to His way of thinking. God lost an entire generation in Israel who were to be the eyewitnesses of His mighty power. They were to tell their children and grandchildren of His glory, so the children might have faith for even greater things, but "their fathers...set not their hearts aright, and whose spirit was not stedfast with God. ...Being armed...turned back in the day of battle. They kept not the covenant...and refused to walk in His law" (Ps. 78:8-10).

We have a covenant to walk with God to obtain a land of promises. "If any man draw back, My soul shall have no pleasure in him" (Heb 10:38). Jesus said that "No man, having put his hand to the plough, and looking back, is fit for the kingdom of God" (Luke 9:62). Fear is not an option; again, *fear is not an option.* We are commanded not to worry: "Be careful for nothing; but in every thing by prayer and supplication with thanksgiving let your requests be made known to God" (Phil. 4:6).

Jeanne was coming back from visiting me on a job in northern Alberta. While driving in the passing lane, a sudden rainsquall made the road very slick. She had just come in between two semi trailer trucks coming down the hill and another two coming up when the car began to hydroplane. Jeanne cried out to the Lord as the car went out of control and made two 360-degree spins in the middle of the road in between all the trucks. The next thing she knew, the car had straightened out and was going up the hill in a normal fashion. You can trust God to deliver you even when disaster seems imminent.

Jeremiah was told to prophesy to Ebed-melech that, even though disaster was coming to Jerusalem, he was not to fear, "For I will surely deliver thee, and thou shalt not fall by the sword, but thy life shall be for a prey unto thee: because thou hast put thy trust in Me, saith the Lord" (Jer. 39:18). Trust eliminates fear, and even if we have fear, we can do it afraid. "Whenever I am afraid, I will trust in You. In God (I will praise His word), in God I have put my trust; I will not fear. What can flesh do to me?" (Ps. 56:3-4 NKJV).

The Bible is full of examples of people who trusted God completely. Shadrach, Meshach, and Abed-nego trusted God. They had been taken captive to Babylon as part of the judgment on Israel. The king of Babylon had passed an edict that everyone had to bow down to his statue as unto God. These three men refused and trusted God in their situation. When the heat came from the king to bow to the idol, and their lives were on the line, they felt no need to compromise. Whatever the outcome, it didn't matter. They were committed to trusting God and could boldly reply to the king: "O Nebuchadnezzar, we are not careful to answer thee in this matter. If it be so, our God…is able to deliver us…out of thine hand, O king. But if not…we will not serve thy gods, nor worship the golden image"

(Dan. 3:16–18). Their reply was not very diplomatic, and it got the expected results: the king's fury and a death sentence.

But God intervened! God saved them, *not by keeping them out of the king's furnace,* but by allowing them to go through the fire with no ill effects. Now instead of death, promotion became these men's fate. In the process, God humbled the king, who then said, "Blessed be… God…who hath sent His angel, and delivered His servants that trusted in Him, and have changed the king's word" (Dan. 3:28).

Do you want power and authority? *You might have to go through the fire, but God will walk with you if you trust in Him.* Jeanne had to commit herself into God's keeping when she had bowel cancer. She said to God, "Live or die, I am Yours." You might have to stand alone against formidable odds and put yourself in an untenable position for God, such that, if He doesn't come through, you're finished.

Here's another example: Elijah, whom the Bible says was a man like us, stood against 450 prophets of Baal on Mount Carmel. He trusted that God was going to vindicate Himself and send down fire. Earlier, Elijah had declared to King Ahab, "As the Lord God of Israel lives, before whom I stand, there shall not be dew nor rain these years, except at my word" (1 Kings 17:1 NKJV). The lack of rain was a judgment that came on Israel because they had served other gods. In the third year of the drought, God said to Elijah: "Go, present yourself to Ahab, and I will send rain on the earth" (1 Kings 18:1 NKJV).

God's promise that He would send rain was predicated on the fact that the serving of false gods would stop. Elijah trusted the word and recognized the conditions required to fulfill it. He stood in proxy for the nation and asked forgiveness for their sins. He then could be fearless and call for God to send down fire and give a demonstration of His power that would be necessary, to change the heart of the nation in a day (see 1 Kings 17–18).

God is going to do even greater wonders than this, Jesus promised, but we must determine in our hearts to say like Job, "Though He slay me, yet will I trust Him" (Job 13:15). Our reliance on anything other than God must be broken, or else those things will continually rise up and short circuit the power that God wants us to operate in.

The first and most important alternate source to break is our reliance upon ourselves. Paul had to break his own reliance and could say, "We had this sentence of death in ourselves, that we should not trust in ourselves, but in God which raises the dead" (2 Cor. 1:9). I had a reliance on a job that I thought would fulfill me. A company wanted to hire me for a position to look after some curtain wall construction (the glass and aluminum fascia on office towers) in England. This job fed into my pride, and I could see myself as being very important. The problem was: my wife had a word from the Lord that the job was not going to work out.

However, I trusted my inflated ego more than I wanted to hear the word of God. I should have recognized my flesh, pushing its own agenda, when tension started to build between

Jeanne and myself. My own pride and ambitions blinded me, and I ignored the signs God was giving. God puts spouses in our lives to bring us back to earth when our pride makes us bigger than we are. The short version of the story is that the company was in trouble with the immigration department as they had broken too many rules bringing foreign workers into the country. They were unable to get me a work visa, so the job never materialized. When flesh gets excited, don't trust yourself; it will just get you into trouble.

Trusting in our own strength (self-reliance) was part of the first great lie. Satan cast doubt (lack of trust) on what God said as being true and mated this doubt with the lie that we could trust our own ability to the point of being like God (see Gen. 3:4-5). Jesus said that we must become like little children to enter the Kingdom of God. Little children trust their parents so completely that, for example, they never worry about what's for supper; they just climb up to the table and wait for it. They have complete faith that supper will appear because they trust in their parents' love for them.

We need to trust God and not our own ability. Here's the key: it is not our ability to hear God but His ability to make us hear. It is not our ability to bring revelation but His ability to shine through us. It is not our ability to see in the spirit realm but His ability to open our eyes. *It's all about Him and what He has done and who He is.* He is able. If we trust Him, we can operate in His power.

God is ever creating, and we need to adjust our thinking to keep up with the revelations He wants to show us. If we trust

God, then the next level He wants to expose to us will not be so scary. It's like teaching a child to swim. If they trust you, then they will jump into the deep end of the pool. If they can't trust, then they will never let go of the side and experience freedom in swimming.

Jeanne has had several experiences where she has seen demonic spirits and Heaven's angels. God then opened her vista a little more by allowing her to encounter some of the saints. We had a doctrinal problem with what she was encountering until God pointed out that Jesus talked with Moses and Elijah on the mount of transfiguration (see Matt. 17). Jesus Himself said that whatever He could do, we could do. We need to trust to be able to walk in these realms.

After we have stopped trusting in our own abilities, we also have to put on the cross all the other things that garner our trust, especially money. When the rich young ruler was invited to join the ranks of the disciples, Jesus put His finger prophetically on the one issue that prevented him from trusting God: his wealth. Jesus loved this young man and wanted him to partake in what was happening. What was waiting for him, a place of authority? Maybe he would have written a book of the Bible. Maybe he would have been one of the early apostles. Certainly his name would have been listed as one of the faithful, but all we hear of him was that he couldn't part with his money, which, for him, had obviously taken the place of trusting Jesus. "Then Jesus…loved him, and said…sell whatsoever thou hast, and give to the poor, and thou shall have treasure in heaven: and come, take up the cross, and follow Me….Jesus… says…how hard is it for them that trust in riches to enter into the kingdom of God" (Mark 10:21,23-24).

I had a dream where I took a quarter out of the return slot in a phone booth. I reached down to pick it up and suddenly was swarmed by a dozen policemen. They arrested me for stealing the quarter. When I woke, God asked me if I was willing to sell my reputation for a quarter. I had in my flesh the nature of a thief, and God was challenging me to repent and deal with this sin in my life. God always knows the strategy of the enemy, and if we trust Him, He will give us the authority to overcome any attacks before they occur. The Bible says, "The love of money is the root of all evil" (1 Tim. 6:10).

James says, "Hath not God chosen the poor of this world rich in faith, and heirs of the kingdom" (James 2:5). Riches are like drugs. They are addictive. God once asked me, "When is enough, enough?" The answer is *never*. If we are dependent on having money, then there is never enough. We always need more. It becomes like a drug addiction, and we need our fix. Unfortunately the fix never fixes the problem, which is fear, fear that God does not really love us enough or have enough power to supply our needs.

The poor, through experience, have learned that God supplies. For them to trust God for the necessities of life is a natural part of being poor. It is not a state that God wants us to remain in, but like everything in life, God can extract some spiritual gold if we have the right attitude and trust. If we just murmur and speak curses and death over our poverty, then we will be stuck with it. If we trust God, then riches or wealth are not necessary, for God will replace it with His abundance, which will supply all our needs in Christ Jesus.

The first major holiday we took with the kids taught us how abundance works. We felt God wanted us to take the kids to Disneyland, but we didn't have much money to fly there. Jeanne found a cheap seat sale, and after prayer, we decided to book the flight. We now felt we needed to pray harder because we had no idea how we were going to pay for the trip. I had just started with a new company as a foreman and was enjoying my work. At Christmas they gave me a bonus, which in construction in those days was unheard of. The bonus more than paid for our trip. I had always been too cheap to allow myself to spend that kind of money on a vacation, but God was training me how to live in abundance.

We can always tell if what we were trusting in was really God or not. God never disappoints. "They cried unto thee, and were delivered: they trusted in You and were not confounded [disappointed]" (Ps. 22:5). So if you have been disappointed, whatever you were trusting in was not God. If a business deal you thought was from God fails and you are disappointed, then your hope and trust were in the business deal not actually in God. If your friends disappoint you, your trust was in your friends and not in God to supply you with friends.

The reason God never disappoints is because we receive by faith from God. Faith is always now, just maybe not yet. That is, faith receives the promise, has it in its possession even though the manifestation in the physical realm may not yet have arrived. That faith, based on a trust in the One who said it, if it is strong, can endure until the promise is seen, even if it takes two weeks, two years, two decades, or two generations to appear. Never disappointed, why? Because we are already in possession of the fulfillment of the promise. "Trust...and He shall bring it to pass" (Ps. 37:5). I have been very disappointed many times. The disappointment usually had to do with investments and was the main tool in overcoming my fleshly desire to get rich. God's ideas always were profitable; profits in my good ideas proved more elusive. I learned to trust God and stop doubting even when I thought I knew better.

Doubt takes our eyes off Jesus and onto the problem. Peter did that when he was walking on the water (see Matt. 14:30). He looked at the wind blowing the sea, and he knew he had a problem. The real problem wasn't the wind and the sea; he was already walking on the water. The real problem was that he doubted, and that made an entrance for fear. Fear is the opposite of faith. It is actually a rejection of the love of God that says, "Love...bears all things, believes all things, hopes all things, endures all things" (1 Cor. 13:7 NKJV). When Peter stopped believing and started doubting, then he had actually stopped allowing the love of God to be expressed through him. He no longer believed all things, nor hoped all things.

Just because Peter couldn't walk on water didn't mean that God couldn't do it for and through him. Jesus had said, "Come," and that should have been enough. But Peter had second thoughts. James calls this being double-minded (of two opinions or literally, two souls). "He that wavers is like a wave of the sea driven with the wind and tossed.... Let not that man think he

200

shall receive any thing of the Lord. A double minded man is unstable in all his ways" (James 1:6-8).

The disciples were tested often on whether they actually believed that what Jesus said would come to pass. Their ability to believe was influenced by their singleness of mind or their double-mindedness. It is the same test that Elijah put out on Mount Carmel: "How long [do you]... halt... between two opinions? If the Lord is God, follow Him: but if Baal, then follow him" (1 Kings 18:21). Double-mindedness then is the opposite of a commitment to God; it is actually an attempt to determine what the most beneficial course is for the person making the decision. That is why changing circumstances will often change our opinion on what may be the best course of action, no matter what we have heard. In other words, our double-mindedness is a fruit of selfishness; what is best for me. The reason our prayers are not answered in those situations is that God will not give us anything (the object of our prayers) that will compete with our affections for Him. God requires a commitment first.

"Delight yourself in the Lord: and He shall give you the desires of your heart. Commit [literally, roll off onto] thy way to the Lord; trust also in Him; and He shall bring it to pass" (Ps. 37:4-5). The commitment will always be tested; if we buckle in unbelief at the first sign of trouble, "if you faint in the day of adversity, thy strength is small" (Prov. 24:10). Jeremiah puts it even more bluntly: "If you have run with the footmen, and they have wearied you, then how can you contend with horses? And if in the land of peace, wherein you trusted, they wearied thee, then how wilt you do in the swelling of Jordan?" (Jer. 12:5).

Jeremiah was trying to get Judah to consider, when even the smallest situation in a time of peace threw them off, what were they going to do when real setbacks in a time of war came along? God is asking you the same question because what you do (your responses) is what you are developing in. If your response is fear and confusion when faced with difficulty, then you are developing in fear and confusion. If your response is faith and confidence, then you are developing faith and confidence.

The ability to trust God in an impossible situation will have already been established by how we reacted to the smaller tests that came into our lives. The more the Kingdom rises up to displace the enemy, the greater will be this resistance. Our strength is no match for satan, but our proper use of authority in the realm God has ordained for us draws Heaven's strength into our situation. Our trust level, as displayed in our thoughts and actions, will determine how much Heaven we will be able to appropriate.

God has taught Jeanne and me to trust the Spirit and how He speaks to our intuition. I remember driving out to visit a couple for dessert and coffee. As we got within one mile of their house, Jeanne started to have this reaction that she didn't want to go there. I argued with her and felt she was just afraid, but she insisted that she felt sick in her spirit. Later we found out that the wife had such fits of anger that on one occasion she had broken her little boy's arm. Jeanne had picked up a spirit of anger but could only feel it, not identify it.

I had the same type of a reaction to a particular man in a wheelchair. I felt unclean and had a hard time being in his presence. We found out afterward that he had been charged with pedophilia.

We also knew a powerful prophet who was making a real impact in the churches in the area. Over time warning bells started to go off, and the Holy Spirit was allowing us to see some of the character flaws in this man. He was too independent to take counsel or correction, and we finally as a church decided to break fellowship with him. It was later that he decided to separate from his wife and take up with his assistant. This flaw in his character concerning sexual purity eventually led him into situations that caused him to be convicted of several sexual misconducts. True authority and discernment will always come from revelation long before there are any facts to back up the feelings. We must be discerning, while at the same time not accusing, if we are going to help each other develop character. Learn to trust the Spirit; He brings wisdom.

"Thou wilt keep him in perfect peace, whose mind is stayed on Thee: because he trusteth in Thee. Trust ye in the Lord for ever: for in the Lord Jehovah is everlasting strength" (Isa. 26:3-4). God is always changing the rules as we move higher into His purposes.[2] He has to do this because as we move into higher realms of spiritual authority we encounter more powerful demons that are in charge of those realms. These are the horses that Jeremiah prophesied we would have to run with.

The disciples had taken their boat out to sea and were struggling, trying to row against the wind. No doubt there was some contention and strife about how to get out of the trouble they found themselves in. There was likely some anger and accusation as to why they were in this situation. The disciples would have been wet and tired and maybe even a little disheartened. When Jesus appeared, walking on the waves, fear also rose up. None of these negative thoughts or words caused the boat to sink. However, when Peter attempted to walk on the water, one thought of fear caused him to sink. In the boat, these thoughts, though not helpful, were not disastrous. On that high place of faith (walking on water), those same thoughts almost killed Peter.

Group dynamics will also elevate the trust response required in a particular situation. When ministry teams or prayer teams are functioning, we need to trust in God and each other to be able to get a victory. God loves to use the Body, and the best way is to have each part of the Body have a part of the solution. That way we need each other to manifest Jesus in each situation.

Peter had demonstrated a strong measure of trust and faith by actually walking on the water (see Matt. 14:29). His lack of trust, displayed by his fear, broke the connection between the word, "Come," which Jesus had spoken to Peter, and Peter's faith, which had allowed that word to operate in his situation. Peter had the word, but "the word...did not profit...not being mixed with faith" (Heb. 4:2). With no mixture of word and faith, Peter sank.

Jesus had already tested the disciples in a very similar situation with another storm. He had said, "Let us go over [to] the other side of the lake" (Luke 8:22). When they got into trouble and the boat was filling with water, they panicked and woke Him up. Jesus' response was "Where is your faith?" He had spoken the word that they were going across and went to sleep, knowing that His word alone was enough to get them across. The disciples trusted more that the storm was going to sink them than that His word would save them. As I have mentioned in a previous chapter, our "boats" are designed to ride out storms, especially with Jesus in the boat. Again, the problem is not when the boat gets in the storm, but when the storm gets in the boat. No peace, and we have no power to rebuke the storm.

The peace was lacking because they didn't understand who Jesus was. They exclaimed, "What manner of man is this...even the winds and waters obey Him" (Luke 8:25). The second time Jesus demonstrated His power over the elements, "The wind ceased...and they...came and worshipped Him, saying...Thou art the Son of God" (Matt. 14:32-33). Jesus was getting them to trust Him, but even after they knew who He was and had confessed it, Peter still had the arrogance to argue with Jesus about how His ministry should look. Peter said, "Thou art the Christ.... And Peter took Him, and began to rebuke Him" (Mark 8:29,32). God knows what is going on. He doesn't need our advice. We can trust Him.

Our trust must eventually result in our complete confidence and obedience. If we think we still know better than God, then we have not really recognized who He is and who we are. In that state, we will be like Job and Peter and will get a rebuke for allowing satan to persuade us that we know better than God. We must check our own responses and see how many times we have arrogantly said no to God's commands. True power and authority will result if we trust God and those He sends to us. "Believe in the Lord your God, so shall you be established; believe His prophets, so shall ye prosper" (2 Chron. 20:20).

God's whole Kingdom is based on God being the ruler and those He has anointed or appointed carrying out His wishes. The Church is "built upon the foundation of the apostles and prophets, Jesus Christ Himself being the chief corner stone; in whom all the building fitly framed together grows unto an holy temple in the Lord: In whom ye also are built together for an habitation of God through the Spirit" (Eph. 2:20-22). We are on a journey to a destination that nobody can properly describe, and we must learn to trust those whom God has placed in charge—else we will end up like the Israelites who constantly grumbled and complained against Moses.

Just recently our pastor, Marc, was heading to Miami with a team to minister in a church there. He asked us to be part of the team. Later, he changed his mind and thought we should stay and look after the church while he was gone. Soon after that, he was back to thinking we should go. We got confused and then realized that the best thing when in confusion is to do what you were doing before you got confused. So we stayed, and I thank God we did. It was after that decision was made that Destiny Image Publishers asked me to have the manuscript for this book ready only six weeks after we would have gotten back from

Miami. During that time, I also had a small maintenance job come up. I believe that our leaders hear for our good, even if they can't articulate what they hear.

The Jewish descendants never learned the lesson of the generation that God abandoned in the wilderness. Years later Israel opted for a plan that the nations around them had adopted: having a king. Though this plan was less than perfect, it mirrored something they could see. Israel had never really embraced God's rule because they never fully trusted Him; they simply obeyed Him.

In Samuel's time they formally rejected God's rule and demanded, "Make us a king to judge us like all the nations" (1 Sam. 8:5). They rejected the unique place God desired them to walk in with Him as their King and Samuel as His prophet. "The Lord said...they have not rejected you, but they have rejected Me, that I should not reign over them" (1 Sam. 8:7). The real reason they wanted a king was so that "our king may judge us, and go out before us, and fight our battles" (1 Sam. 8:20). They were giving up their place of intimacy with God (which gave them authority) and giving it to a king.

The Israelites of Moses' time had done the same thing at Mount Sinai. God spoke the commandments to the people, but they responded by telling Moses, "You speak with us and we will hear, but let not God speak with us, lest we die" (Exod. 20:19). God, through His intimate talking to Moses face to face, was establishing Moses' authority. "Lo, I come...that the people may hear when I speak with you, and believe you for ever" (Exod. 19:9).

Israel didn't trust that God wanted to be intimate with them. They feared Him as a hard taskmaster just as the Egyptians had been. They believed that close contact with God would bring out the lash of discipline. Their fears would not allow them to trust Him. Jesus put His whole trust in God. They taunted Him on the cross (see Matt. 27:43) just as David had prophesied, saying, "He trusted on the Lord that He would deliver Him" (Ps. 22:8). Right from the womb, the Scriptures say, Jesus' spirit leaned on God as His only support. David did likewise: "For I will not trust in my bow, neither shall my sword save me. But Thou hast saved us from our enemies" (Ps. 44:6-7).

God is looking to show Himself strong to those whose trust is in Him. That strength manifests itself to the world as power and authority in our lives.

ENDNOTES

1. K.C. Tessendorf, "White Knuckles over Niagara," http://www.highliteskids.com.

2. See Appendix A.

Chapter 6

The Key to Strength—Joy

THE JOY OF THE LORD IS YOUR STRENGTH

Joy is not happiness. The word *happiness* comes from the Icelandic and Middle English word *happenstance*, which is also the root word for *chance*.[1] So happiness depends on chance or circumstances. For example, I am happy because the sun is shining or the boss gave me a raise or somebody complimented me. *Joy*, on the other hand, is an expression of the fruit of the Spirit. It means "to brighten" and usually is expressed with an accompanying action: shouting, spinning, leaping, that comes out of a violent emotion. The circumstances can be devastating, and joy can still be present.

The prophet Habakkuk composed a poem that expressed how joy works:

Although the fig tree shall not blossom, neither shall fruit be in the vines; the labour of the olive shall fail, and the fields yield no meat [food]; *the flocks shall be cut off from the fold, and there shall be no herd in the stalls. Yet I will rejoice in the Lord, I will joy in the God of my salvation. The Lord God is my strength, and He will make my feet like hinds' feet, and He will make me to walk upon mine high places* (Habakkuk 3:17-19).

The prophet had just seen the vision of an impending destructive invasion, yet he understood that rejoicing in God, not fearing the circumstances, was the way to gain personal strength and to have the ability to rise above those circumstances.

Though the following story is a minor incident compared to the life-changing invasion that Habakkuk was facing, it illustrates the principle. I was involved in a strongman and skills competition called the King of the Klondike. One of the events was a log-chopping contest. Each man had a 13-inch, vertically positioned log to chop. I was first up and set to go head to head against the world champion log chopper. I thought that I was going to be taught a lesson because his credentials were impressive. As he marked up his log to facilitate his chop, I became even more certain that my doom was imminent. I decided to just give it my best shot and let the chips fall where they would.

Slowly I started to feel a joy coming up within me, and by the time we lined up to chop, I knew I was going to have fun. The signal went off, and we tied into our logs. The way we were facing allowed me a view of my opponent, while he had his back to me. God must have guided my ax because every cut was true and deep. Huge chips flew out, and on the 13th stroke, I was through my tree. I had time to drop my ax to the ground and assume a posture of leaning on the handle before my opponent finished his last swing and checked to see how I was doing. I have to say, my joy was showing through as I saw the incredulous look on his face. The joy that rose up in me was the factor that overcame the fear that confronted me.

The circumstances God arranges are not designed to destroy you but rather to enable you to gain victory over them. You achieve victory over circumstances not by having the ability to change the circumstances for your advantage, but rather by using the circumstances to expose any hooks in you. Satan gets hooks in us in any area where we have unhealed wounds. Those places have not been submitted to God (as evidenced by their unhealed nature), and the enemy therefore has the right of access. The enemy has no authority on this earth except when we yield our authority to him. When society as a whole yields to satan, then he wields great power, but not over us.

Jesus told His disciples, "I give you power to tread on serpents and scorpions, and over all the power of the enemy: and nothing shall by any means hurt you" (Luke 10:19). Later He said, "They shall lay their hands on you, and persecute you, delivering you up to the synagogues, and into prisons, being brought before kings and rulers for My name's sake...and it shall turn to you for a testimony" (Luke 21:12-13). Jesus was trying to make us understand that hard times are coming, but that we should not panic. Our *response* dictates what the outcome will be, *not* the *circumstances* that assail us. We are not going to be able stop the enemy from coming against us, but we will be able to stop the enemy. God's purpose is to give us a testimony.

Fear is a spirit, but joy is a fruit of the Spirit. Joy is part of our perfected love package and is designed to destroy fear. It tells the enemy that you already know the outcome and are going to enjoy watching it all unfold. Part of the way that Jeanne and I declare our trust in God for our provision is to give away much more than our tithe. It is a joy to express our confidence in God and to participate in the Kingdom, no matter what is happening.

Jesus went on to say, "And you shall be betrayed...and some...shall...be put to death. But there shall not an hair on your head perish" (Luke 21:16,18). Aren't those opposing statements? *Put to death—not a hair perish.* How can we be preserved and yet die? Earlier, after He had given the disciples power, Jesus said, "Rejoice not, that the spirits are subject to you; but rather rejoice, because your names are written in Heaven" (Luke 10:20). Jesus was trying to cast their eyes beyond the circumstances. *Don't get excited when you seem to win; don't get excited when you seem to lose.* Why? Because it's not about winning and losing in this realm—else Jesus would have made sure He won every conflict. He was interested only in the spiritual realm for He knew the natural would always mirror the spiritual. He told Pilate before His crucifixion, "If My Kingdom were of this world, then would My servants fight" (John 18:36).

Jesus was saying to the 12, "You have already won. You have gained your entrance to Heaven. Now operate from that heavenly realm like I do. Be willing to die and release those still captive, and rejoice in the victory even as satan flails against you. He has no more power over you." They got what He was saying. Soon after His resurrection and after their filling with the Spirit, Peter and John were beaten. Their response was that they "rejoiced that they were counted worthy to suffer shame for His name" (Acts 5:41).

I have had to take verbal beatings by people who wanted to blame me for all the problems that happened to them. The local church I was attending was going through a major shift in the way we were worshiping and in our authority structure. Almost two-thirds of the congregation was in favor of more radical worship, but it was hard for the others to adapt. When some of the families decided to go to a more traditional church, a lot of wounding resulted. Satan is always trying to put people at odds with each other. The trick is not to worry about whether a battle is won or lost but about whether I allowed offense to come into my heart. I was glad to be the one who got attacked, as I know it prevented others from getting hurt. That joy in the battle was the grace of God.

The disciples experienced the same grace. Only weeks before their beating, they were hiding in fear. Now they had made a decision that the same attacks, which they had feared, were something to rejoice about. That joy was released by an act of their will.

David showed this attitude in the Psalms, "Why are you cast down, O my soul? Why are you disquieted in me? Hope in thou in God: for I shall yet praise Him" (Ps. 42:5). David realized that his intimate relation to God was reason enough to get excited, no matter what else was going on. This joy comes from the indwelling of the Spirit and is not something that we work up. We don't put on a "happy face" or "whistle in the dark" to work something up. It is part of who the Spirit in us is.

John the Baptist, while still in his mother's womb, had joy. Elisabeth said, "As soon as...thy salutation sounded in [my] ears, the babe [John] leaped in my womb for joy" (Luke 1:44). It had been prophesied that John would be filled with the Holy Ghost even from the womb. John's spirit responded because the Holy Spirit in him responded to the presence of God in Jesus. Nothing worked up, nothing contrived, just pure joy empowered John and allowed him to leap.

I have had that bubble of joy come over me quite often, sometimes at work, sometimes standing in a grocery line. It may send a shiver through me, cause me to twitch, or just brighten my whole being, but it always catches me by surprise. It's like my wife sneaking up on me and giving me a tickle.

When Jeanne was eight, she used to go to church all by herself. Her parents weren't Christians; God just drew her. One Easter Sunday she got all dressed up and went to church. Coming home from the service, her spirit leapt up within her. It was like her spirit almost went right out of her, it got so excited. She skipped all the way home. That experience kept drawing her to find the source of that joy. It would be 12 years before she finally found Jesus who had caused her spirit to leap just like John the Baptist's spirit had done centuries before.

Joy is present because the Spirit is present, and if we allow it to, joy will bubble up as we allow it freedom for expression. This is just one expression of the Kingdom. "For the kingdom of God is not meat and drink; but righteousness, and peace, and joy in the Holy Ghost" (Rom. 14:17). All three of these aspects of the Kingdom came as a result of the Holy Ghost's being present and being given the place of Lord in each situation. They are not a result of our effort to produce these attributes of the Holy Spirit in our souls.

Our attitude must conform to God's attitude. We are to conform to Christ's image, so we must also mirror His responses. When it seems as though all hell is coming against us, we must ask ourselves, "What would Jesus do?" David saw in the spirit "the kings...and rulers take counsel... against the Lord, and His anointed...He that sits in the heavens shall laugh:...the Lord shall have them in derision" (Ps. 2:2,4). As Christians we can't look at the problems in the world as something to wring our hands about. God's response is to laugh. We must take the same attitude and let joy rule instead of allowing fear to be our response.

Real entrepreneurs don't fear when the economy goes bad; instead, they learn to profit from it. As Christians we need that same entrepreneurial attitude, not in the financial sense but in the spiritual. God knows that hard times stir up people to act, even if it is because they have nothing left to lose. If the Church can posture itself to help these people who are going through hard times, they can both manifest the love of God and add disciples to the Kingdom. If we let the Spirit rule, He will respond with His character through us.

"The wicked plot against the just…The Lord shall laugh at him: for He sees that his day is coming" (Ps. 37:12-13). We have a tendency to cry, whine, and bemoan our "fate" rather than claim our destiny and say, "What can man do unto me?" (Ps. 118:6). Our joy is to agree with God and do the opposite of what everybody else is doing. Murmuring and complaining shows a lack of understanding, but joy agrees with God's point of view.

Isaiah could see what God was doing when the king of Assyria was besieging Jerusalem and threatening their lives. The Jews had no power to resist, but God declared His thoughts toward the king of Assyria. "This is the word the Lord has spoken concerning him; The virgin the daughter of Zion hath despised [you], and laughed [you] to scorn" (2 Kings 19:21).

God said, "The daughters of Jerusalem laughed at Sennacherib." They weren't laughing yet, but they would be. Prophecy declares what is now, just not yet. There are no time restraints in the Spirit realm. We are always in a panic when things are going badly, but situations don't dictate results. The word of God dictates results. If we "live by every word that is proceeding from the mouth of God" (Matt. 4:4), then we can laugh at circumstances.

In this incident concerning the king of Assyria, God spoke; Isaiah declared it; and "The angel of the Lord…smote 185,000 and…they were all dead corpses" (2 Kings 19:35). When we know the power of God and the joy that He has watching over us, then no matter what the enemy tries to do, we will not fear.

Once when Jeanne's mom was praying, one of her sons came to mind. She phoned Jeanne saying that she couldn't pray for him without crying. Jeanne started to pray, and the same thing happened. Rather than interceding until God showed them what was going on, they stayed in this depressed crying mood. Jeanne's brother ended up falling off the steel the next day but miraculously missed a whole row of rebar that was right below him. He landed in the dirt, ten feet from where he should have, and only broke his foot. His foreman had told him to tighten up the laces on his boots, which likely saved even further injury.

Knowing the plans of the enemy will not bring fear if we can have joy in anticipation of what God is going to do. If all we can see or feel is the pain and fear, we will not be able to intercept the enemy's plans. We need to find God's will in every situation so that we can laugh when God promises the impossible.

Sarah laughed when God said she would have a baby. It caught her so off guard that a bubble of joy just escaped out while she was eavesdropping on what the Lord was saying to her husband. No wonder she laughed; she was 90 years old when the promise was given. God challenged her, "Why did Sarah laugh...is anything too hard for the Lord" (Gen. 18:13-14). That joy was the empowering of the Holy Spirit and resulted in the birth of Isaac. *Isaac* means "laughter,"[2] so the first fruit of the "Father of Faith" (Abraham) was laughter at what God can do in the face of the impossible.

Over the course of many years, God has allowed Jeanne and me to minister to hundreds of people, some of them in bad shape. It has always been exciting to watch God step into situations that seem beyond repair and create a miracle. The joy of knowing that God is able to change all circumstances will erupt in songs of deliverance.

This is part of what worship is supposed to be. It is to be a statement of faith mixed with joy and expectation. Paul and Silas experienced what praise and worship could do for people in prison. "At midnight Paul and Silas prayed, and sang praises to God...Suddenly there was a great earthquake...and immediately all the doors were opened, and every one's bands were loosed" (Acts 16:25-26). The remarkable part of this story is that Paul and Silas had been falsely accused and beaten before they were thrown into prison and chained up in the lowest dungeon. They were filled with joy because they were anticipating deliverance and a reward for their trouble. The jailer was so astounded by the power God displayed and the attitude of Paul and Silas that "he...rejoiced...believing in God, with all his house" (Acts 16:34). Songs of deliverance must be accompanied by an attitude of joy that displays the expectation of that deliverance.

On the way out of Egypt, it wasn't until after the parting of the Red Sea and the drowning of all the Egyptians that the Israelites expressed any joy. They still had a slave mentality, and even their music was slave music with no joy. When Miriam led the women in a triumphant dance, the joy expressed brought a certain amount of freedom. Yet because the nation could not escape its slave roots and attitudes, those who left Egypt never fully entered into a joyful expectation of what God had promised them. All they ever saw was the wilderness, and they could never look beyond it to see the freedom. Their hearts never knitted to the Lord but stayed hard and stubborn; therefore after ten tests (see Num. 14:22), God said "enough" and rejected them. If we do not incorporate joy into our walk with God, then we too will just experience a wilderness in our lives.

God went to the next generation and started to prepare them for the rigors of war. This was a people raised in the wilderness but in freedom. They had time and again watched God come through and had been raised in worship and the re-counting of the exploits of God's mighty deeds in Egypt. To combat one final outbreak of murmuring, God allowed a plague of snakes into the camp. God's judgment was tempered with mercy as Moses was told to raise up a brass serpent on a pole to counteract the bites of the serpents (see Num. 21:6,8).

Jesus later referred to this symbolic representation of Him-self on the cross: "Even as Moses lifted up the serpent in the wilderness, even so must the Son of Man be lifted up" (John 3:14). We even use that symbol today as a healing symbol for the medical profession.

Once the plague of poisonous snakes ended, from that point on Israel entered into war, but the murmuring ceased. An attitude of faith emerged. The next time they needed water, they didn't complain, but rather, "Israel sang this song, Spring up, O well; sing ye unto it" (Num. 21:17). Joy in the midst of difficulties had emerged, and that paved the way for the victories to come. They were now ready for war.

God had known from the beginning that their fathers couldn't fight. God did not lead them through the land of the Philistines, although it was nearly an 11-day journey. "Lest...the people repent when they see war and...return to Egypt" (Exod. 13:17). The joy they released gave them authority to deal with real enemies.

Jesus told His disciples, "I give...you power to tread on serpents and scorpions, and over all the power of the enemy: and nothing shall...hurt you.... [However] in this rejoice not, that the spirits are subject unto you; but rather rejoice, because your names are written in Heaven" (Luke 10:19-20).

I remember in one ministry session Jeanne and I were dealing with a young lady who had a powerful ministry herself, but she got depressed quite often. As we ministered, looking for roots, I saw a demon manifest. I looked into her eyes, and the thing threatened me. The demon said, "I'm going to kill you." I knew my God, and I was not about to let a demon threaten me. "Oh, no, you won't!" I said as I stared back at the demon. Immediately the threatening posture turned to fear, and the lady ran around to the other side of the table.

It was only a short time later when we got her to repent for cooperating with a spirit of fear, and she commanded the spirit out of herself.[3] The joy then erupted in the room as we danced in God's victory. Never again did that lady come under demonic attack that she could not repel with joy. In fact, now her husband says to her jokingly, "Less joy," whenever she gets too excited. Our real source of joy is in knowing our place, seated in the heavenlies with God. Out of that realm comes our power over the enemy. Therefore our victories will only come as the assurance of that fact enters our hearts. That assurance will result in joy in the face of difficulties or even the enemy himself. Then the Lord becomes our strength and song.

The relationship between rejoicing and our position in Christ is emphasized in the Scripture, "Christ...whose we are, if we hold fast the confidence and the rejoicing of the hope firm unto the end" (Heb. 3:6). If we are sure of His care, then that joy will allow us to function like Jesus. In the Old Testament, God instructed Israel to keep their joy in all situations. This world is full of poor and needy people.

Sometimes all the problems we see tend to overwhelm us, and we can get upset at having to look after the demands that are placed on us. At those times, even doing something like looking after the poor can seem like a burden, but God wants us so filled with hope and joy that we can respond to needs in like manner. "God loves a cheerful [hilarious] giver" (2 Cor. 9:7). Jeanne and I get excited when we give to the Lord. We know that God is going to use that money to change people's lives. If we think there is a limited supply, then we will fear giving away what we might need ourselves. If we know that we are dipping from an endless well, then there is freedom to give.

To be able to act like this, we must have the mind of Christ so that we can think like Him. We can then respond differently, even to those who attack us. God has big shoulders. He is not offended by people who are angry with Him. God has given a gift of mercy into His Body, but He wants us to have

His attitude in operating that gift. He wants those who show mercy to do it with cheerfulness (see Rom. 12:8).

No more duty! That is the essence of joy, for duty is the opposite of joy. Duty is work done grudgingly. Duty is religion, and God will not receive anything from us because we "have" to do it. God wants us to give with joy in every area of our lives. Any other type of giving is just duty, and God hates "duty attitude." Duty is a lukewarm response, and God says that if we are "lukewarm...I will spew you out of My mouth" (Rev. 3:16).

Think of it in terms of intimacy within a marriage. If this act of love has deteriorated to duty on the part of one of the partners, the other will not even want to respond. Their conversation will go like this, "If you are just going to do it because you have to, don't bother. Go sleep on the couch." God portrays Himself as a jealous lover who wants some passion in the relationship. We are told to "serve the Lord with gladness: come before His presence with singing" (Ps. 100:2). Any other response will be rejected.

This is what He said to Isaiah: "This people draw near Me with their mouth, but have removed their heart far from Me" (Isa. 29:13). If our hearts are not right, we will have no joy; and if we have no joy, God will not accept us. If we have no acceptance, there is no covenant, and thus no power. Joy is our precursor for power.

In the natural realm, joy and laughter are designed by God to empower health. "A merry heart does good like a medicine: but a broken spirit dries the bones" (Prov. 17:22). I fell while at work a few years ago. We had been preparing for a shutdown at a fertilizer plant and had removed several floors of steel. In the process of putting this steel back in the plant, I had stepped through a hole. I fell, about 20 feet, to the grating floor below. There were several large holes within a few feet of where I landed, and had I rolled into one of those I would have gone another 70 feet to the ground.

God had been speaking to me about slowing down, and as I lay on that grating, I heard Him say, "So stop." I knew exactly what He meant. I repented right there for not listening to Him and asked Him to forgive me. All of a sudden I started to laugh. The laughter came from deep in my spirit and convulsed through my body. I had to suppress the outward manifestation of that laughter as the paramedics got ready to transport me to the hospital. I didn't want them to think I was delirious or completely crazy.

I was, after all, seriously injured. Falling through the grating hole, I had ripped up my side, split open my head, broken one wrist, and injured my knee. When I landed, I broke one foot, broke the other wrist (in 12 places), and bruised my back. The gash over my forehead was bleeding profusely and created a big pool of blood around me on some fire blankets that we had laid down earlier. I looked quite a mess and was in lots of pain, but I couldn't stop laughing with the joy of the Lord. I believe that my joy, along with the Lord's placement of a bone surgeon in the emergency ward that particular day, healed my bones. Even with all the damage, this doctor was able to realign the bones in my wrist and, without surgery or pins, set them in place. The surgeon who attended me during my recovery said that it was amazing that, with so many bone fractures, I would not need any surgery.

We need to laugh; it is healthy. *Life may be rough, but God is good.* Get a funny movie; tell some jokes with friends; remember some crazy situations you have gone through. The act of laughing releases endorphins that aid in the healing process. As Christians we need to loosen up and enjoy this life that God has created for us. God wants us to be childlike in our response to His presence. "Let Israel rejoice in Him that made him: let the children of Zion be joyful in their King" (Ps. 149:2).

We can respond with this joy because we know the end—not just the end here but also the end of our journey with Christ. Isaiah, speaking of the millennial reign of Christ, ends with this verse: "The ransomed of the Lord shall return, and come to Zion with songs and everlasting joy upon their heads: they shall obtain joy and gladness, and sorrow and sighing shall flee away" (Isa. 35:10). If we have this hope and faith, let us show it in our joy no matter what the circumstances.

Nehemiah declares the same thing to the people returning from Babylonian captivity. The people were weeping and crying as Ezra read the word of the law to them. Nehemiah said, "This day is holy unto our Lord: neither be ye sorry; for the joy of the Lord is your strength" (Neh. 8:10).

My wife likes to joke that the joy of shopping is her strength. It's true; when we go out shopping, I power out right away, but she is having so much fun that she can go on for hours. Women's clothing stores could sell a lot more if they would supply chairs in their stores for the men who are not experiencing as much joy as their wives are while shopping. Joy brings seemingly endless power.

We are told to "Rejoice in the Lord always: and again I say, Rejoice" (Phil. 4:4). Why? It's all about God and about what He did, not about our circumstances. We can rejoice because He conquered. We can rejoice because He saved us. The feasts of Israel were physical examples for us of how we are to respond to God. These holy days were to be days of celebration. The Day of Atonement was the only time they were to grieve over their sins and to not express joy before their God. All the rest were days of feasting, which lasted a week. They were invitations for us to rejoice and celebrate.

Psalm 100 commands us, "Make a joyful noise unto the Lord. Serve the Lord with gladness: come before His presence with singing" (Ps. 100:1-2). We often look upon these statements as suggestions, not commands. Jesus never asked anyone to do anything. He always gave commands; either do it or not, obey or disobey. The Ten Commandments are not the Ten Suggestions. God doesn't even say we can worship the Lord in our own way, like we often placate people with. Jesus commands us to worship God's way, in spirit and in truth, but also in joy. God told Israel, "Because you did not serve the Lord your God with joyfulness, and with gladness of heart, for the abundance of all things; shall you serve your enemies...in hunger...in thirst...in nakedness and in the want of all things" (Deut. 28:47-48).

The command is: serve God with joy or your enemies with sorrow! As with all God's commands, the punishment that comes when we disobey is a consequence of our choice. Without joy there will be no strength or faith to repel the enemy. The result of that reduced strength will be captivity. The joy of the Lord is our strength, and that strength allows us to overcome the lies of the enemy.

The devil often comes to the people of God with the lie that all the church or preacher wants is your money. We need to hold onto our money lest someone steal it. That is a lie. Jesus said, "Lay up for yourselves, treasures in heaven... where thieves do not...steal" (Matt. 6:20). Tithing is something to get excited about. It is part of our covenant: we tithe and He protects and supplies. That should bring great joy that we no longer have to supply for ourselves.

Psalm 19:5 states, "Rejoice as a strong man to run a race." It is a joy to operate from a realm of strength. Strong people like to work out and push the limits of their strength. Olympic quality athletes are always pushing for personal bests. Spiritual warriors love to encounter the enemy and displace him from people's lives. When we stay in joy, we can stay in God's presence and in His purposes. We can act like Him even in the presence of our enemies, for God is not worried by those opposed to Him and neither should we be. "But Thou, O Lord, shall laugh at them; Thou shalt have all the heathen in derision. Because of His strength will I wait upon Thee: for God is my defense" (Ps. 59:8-9).

All suggestion of fear is disbanded when the Father is with us. Even a doctor's negative reports should not faze us. A doctor told Jeanne a long time ago that she needed a hysterectomy.

She consulted with Jesus who is our "great physician," and He told her she didn't. So she never had one and never needed one. "The Lord is my strength and my shield; my heart trusted in Him, and I am helped: …my heart greatly rejoiceth" (Ps. 28:7). Trust God and rejoice in His goodness.

(This is not to suggest that you should not take your doctor's advice; for they too were given by God. But in this case, Jeanne had an indisputable word from the Lord that she acted upon through faith and assurance.)

God will allow persecution and hatred to arise against us, but Jesus said, "Blessed are you, when men shall revile you, and persecute you, and shall say all manner of evil against you falsely, for My sake. Rejoice, and be exceeding glad: for great is your reward in heaven: for so persecuted they the prophets" (Matt. 5:11-12). Now I don't know anybody who actually is happy when people express their hatred toward them. The point is that it's not happiness or a good feeling that dictates joy. It's an attitude that we must learn to cultivate, and the only way it is learned is through trials: "Count it all joy when you fall into various temptations; knowing this, that the testing of your faith worketh [produces] patience. But let patience have its perfect work, that you may be perfect and entire, lacking nothing" (James 1:2-4).

God is preparing us to walk with Him in authority. When I was going to the university, I sometimes had to study for days for exams. It was a lot of work, but once the exam actually arrived, the work was over. All I had to do was to write down what I had worked so hard to learn. Training is designed to be harder than the actual test. The practices which I endured playing football were much more grueling than the games. The coaches did it that way so that the opposition could not intimidate us. We were not only gaining muscles; we were gaining heart.

The principle is: "Though our outward man perish, yet the inward man is renewed day by day" (2 Cor. 4:16). We must shift from our carnal nature and step back in our spiritual nature to be able to rejoice at what is happening: "For our light affliction…[works] for us a far more exceeding and eternal weight of glory" (2 Cor. 4:17). In other words, in trials, the spirit man gets multiplied more than the carnal man does. What do we want? Do we want to be like Jesus or to have a comfortable life? If we are truly letting Jesus live in us, then the same type of situations will confront our body and soul as those that confronted Jesus' body and soul when He was in them.

We must learn to embrace the situations God brings to us because they alone will kill the old nature and allow us to operate in God's nature. That is why Paul could say, "Most gladly therefore will I rather glory in my infirmities, that the power of Christ may rest upon me" (2 Cor. 12:9).

Jeanne suffered with fibromyalgia for years. Sometimes it would be so bad that it would keep her in bed all day. She could hardly comb her hair. We prayed about it and got no specific answer of how to combat this chronic, debilitating condition. As we got ourselves more healed up inwardly and started forgiving others, our joy in life started to increase. As I became more loving toward Jeanne and she was able to release me from her judgments against me, though we cannot say for sure that this was the reason, she was healed from fibromyalgia. No sudden change but a total healing. Now she is more active than she was 15 years ago and feels no weakness. We can all suffer in our situations, but God does not intend to leave us there.

The psalmist knew this secret when he said, "Weeping may endure for a night, but joy comes in the morning" (Ps. 30:5). A couple who is very dear to us experienced both the night and the morning that the psalmist referred to. The husband, because of a lack of love in his childhood, could not love himself; and for comfort, he ended up having an affair. It was devastating for everyone involved. The husband moved in with the other woman for a few days and would not receive any correction. All we could do was to pray.

He came back on a Sunday, and I was able to talk with him. All I could do was to speak some truth about how God hated divorce. I told him that God would back him right up to the edge of hell if necessary to get him to turn around. Others in the Body spoke some tough love as well, and he decided to come home. The problem with sexual contact with another is that soul ties develop. Even though he was home, for months he was playing the game of deciding where he wanted to be: stay home or go with the other woman. He slowly slipped back into his fantasy of another life and again decided to leave his wife.

At that point, with nothing else to lose, his wife put down her foot and gave him the ultimatum: either *her* or *me and the kids*. This seemed to shock him enough to change his mind and try to make the marriage work. He went for counseling and also came to Jeanne and me. We went after the roots, and through repentance, he started on the long road back.

There is a little aside to this story that God plopped in our laps. The girlfriend from this affair contacted us and wanted a meeting. She was still attached to the husband because of her soul ties, but God gave us compassion and wisdom. Before the night was over, she had repented of her part in the adultery and also had given her life to the Lord! She contacted us about a year and a half later and said that she had gone through an Alpha course and was well established in a church. She wanted to thank us for what we had done.

Our friends' marriage continued to grow back to health, and I can say that they have recovered. That was seven years ago. What started out as a night of tears, God turned into a day of rejoicing.

God wasn't just saying that eventually the problems would go away, but rather that as we endure and are changed, then the light (the revelation of God's will) will dawn on us and we will see clearly what is transpiring. Paul learned this lesson and could proclaim, "I am exceedingly joyful in all our tribulation" (2 Cor. 7:4). He was mimicking Jesus, who "for the joy that was set before Him endured the cross" (Heb. 12:2). We can endure because we know the joy that is coming.

Jeanne and I minister to all the people that we do because we know the joy that both they and God will have with their deliverance. That gives us strength to carry on. We are told to "consider Him that endured such contradiction of sinners against Himself, lest you be wearied and faint in your minds. You have not yet resisted unto blood, striving against sin" (Heb. 12:3-4).

The endurance or the failure that we accomplish is in our minds: in our thought life and our attitudes. The battle is in your mind, but that battle takes on flesh and bones when it touches the things we have accumulated or the people we hold dear. Satan's boast to God against Job was, "Put forth Your hand now, and touch all that he has, and he will curse You to Your face" (Job 1:11 AMP). He was saying to God, "They only serve You for what they get."

New Testament believers proved satan wrong. The writer of Hebrews is commending the Christians that they "took joyfully the spoiling of [their] goods, knowing...in heaven [they have] a better and an enduring substance" (Heb. 10:34). These Christians had rejoiced at being robbed of their stuff. Why could they act like that? Because they knew the Scriptures that said, "If the thief be found, let him pay double" (Exod. 22:7). If we really believe that Scripture, then we won't flip out when everything seems to be going badly. We can be assured that whatever the devil attempts to steal from us, God will force him to pay us back double as compensation.

The proof of our belief—that God is just and will look after us—is our joy. I can give something away joyfully if I know that it is going to be replaced by something better. Jeanne's brother applauded our lifestyle and hope when he remarked, "If you win, you win; if you lose, you still win." Let's rejoice in the Lord because He is good!

231

We are told that God will give us "the oil of joy for mourning, the garment of praise for the spirit of heaviness...that He might be glorified" (Isa. 61:3). God is glorified by our praise. That causes us to praise even more: "I will greatly rejoice in the Lord, my soul shall be joyful in my God; for He has clothed me with the garments of salvation, He has covered me with the robe of righteousness" (Isa. 61:10).

Knowing this we can "rejoice evermore" (1 Thess. 5:16). Nature itself rejoices with us: "You shall go out with joy...the mountains and the hills shall break forth before you into singing, and all the trees of the field shall clap their hands" (Isa. 55:12). All nature is waiting for us to come into our destiny as the children of God. God is going to teach us how to walk in the glory that is coming. "Be glad then, you children of Zion, and rejoice in the Lord your God: for He has given you the former rain moderately, and he will cause to come down for you the rain, the former rain, and the latter rain..." (Joel 2:23). Just as rain refreshes and feeds or nourishes the earth, God is giving us teaching to train us how to rightly live, showers of words to feed and refresh the soul. Those teachers will often be our circumstances. We need to embrace all that our loving Father sends our way. Someone once said, what doesn't kill us will only make us stronger. No matter what happens, we can rejoice if we believe that.

ENDNOTES

1. *Webster's Twentieth Century Dictionary*, s.v.v. "Happy" (hap, happe, good luck, chance), "Happen" (happe: Ice. happ, chance, luck).

2. Alfred Jones, *Jones Dictionary of Old Testament Proper Names* (Grand Rapids, MI: Kregel Publications, 1997), s.v. "Isaac."

3. See Appendix B.

Chapter 7

The Gift That Keeps on Giving—Love

GOD IS LOVE

Love is the language of Heaven. The Father, Son, and Holy Spirit have a deep devotion to and affection for one another. They are continually deferring to each other, respecting, esteeming, and praising one another. They are in perfect harmony, of one mind and heart. They are the supreme example of intimacy and love.

The Father honors the Son by declaring that "at the name of Jesus every knee should bow" (Phil. 2:10). The Son honors the Father by exalting Him. Jesus responded to someone who called Him good with the statement, "Why call...Me good? There is none good but one, that is, God" (Matt. 19:17). Both

Father and Son honor the Holy Spirit's position by declaring that "he that shall blaspheme against the Holy Ghost hath never forgiveness" (Mark 3:29). Both Jesus and the Holy Spirit take on the nature of servants, and the Holy Spirit submits to Jesus by coming in Jesus' name and bringing to the disciples' remembrance all of the things that Jesus said (see John 14:26). Jesus also says that the Helper shall "not speak of Himself; but whatsoever He shall hear, that shall He speak" (John 16:13). That is perfect harmony and submission. Each has a role to play, and each gladly functions in that role for the mutual benefit of the others.

Paul says that the relationship between Christ and His Church is to be a mirror of that model, as is marriage.

> *Submitting yourselves one to another in the fear of God. Wives, **submit** yourselves unto your own husbands, as unto the Lord. For the husband is the head of the wife, even as Christ is the head of the church: and He is the savior of the body. Therefore as the church is **subject** unto Christ, so let the **wives be** to their own husbands **in every thing**. Husbands, **love** your wives, even as Christ also loved the church, and gave Himself for it; that He might sanctify and cleanse it with the washing of water by the word, that He might present it to Himself a glorious church, not having spot, or wrinkle, or any such thing; but that it should be holy and without blemish. So ought men to love their wives as their own bodies. He that **loveth** his wife loveth himself. For no man ever yet hated his own flesh; but nourisheth and cherisheth it, even as the Lord the church: for we are members of His body, of His flesh,*

and of his bones. For this cause shall a man leave his fa-
ther and mother, and shall be joined unto his wife, and
they two shall be one flesh. This is a great mystery: but I
speak concerning Christ and the church. Nevertheless let
every one of you in particular so love his wife even as
himself; and the wife see that she reverence her husband
(Ephesians 5:21-33).

Four times in this passage, the husband is told to love his
wife, and the wife is told three times to come under or reverence her husband. God uses the home environment to create
the character in us that will allow us to function in the Kingdom and defeat the enemy. It is often difficult for a man to
take his headship in a loving manner. When Jeanne went into
the hospital for her cancer operation, she and I agreed that I
needed to be there all the time that I could. For the next nine
days, I stayed an average of 12 hours a day, every day. I fetched
water, adjusted pillows, rubbed her feet and back, prayed for
her, sang to her, and just generally covered and protected her.
This was my wife; she needed me, and I was putting everything aside to show her love. It took nearly nine months for
her to fully recover, and I carried the weight of the house as
much as I could. We joked that, because she had supported me
through my last year of university, I would have to support
her for the next 40 years. I think I got the best of the deal.

It is often just as difficult for a woman to submit in a loving
manner. These positions do not indicate worth; they indicate
function. The family function is designed to teach the next
generation how the Godhead functions. It is also a statement,

into the spiritual realm, that both physically and spiritually God's wisdom works. The honor and respect that a husband and wife display toward each other and their children is the training material the kids need to manage their own lives. Children come into this world totally self-centered and selfish, and they need this attitude to change if they are to be useful members of society and the Kingdom of God. Mom and dad train their children how to operate in respect, honor, love, and faith through modeling these things amongst the family members.

The opposite of this love is selfishness. We defeat selfishness by coming in the opposite spirit, that is, by being loving. If Jeanne acts totally lovingly toward me, I am too embarrassed to consistently act like a jerk toward her. As she grows in love, my growth in selfishness becomes woefully obvious.

We made arrangements once to sell our van to some acquaintances. We were taking a position with World Vision and would not need the vehicle. Later, God spoke to us, and we decided to decline the offer. Our friends, however, would not let us out of the deal for the van. We could have said, "Sorry, we've changed our minds," but God said that we were to keep our word, even if it seemed like it would hurt us (see Ps. 15:4). Our friends displayed their selfishness by looking after their desires, so now we needed to go out and buy a new van. God supplied a luxury van, fully loaded with over $13,000 of extras, for a very cheap price. That van lasted 15 years. Even when people act selfishly toward us, if we come in the opposite spirit, God can bless us and allow us to grow in His love.

We are always developing in whatever seed is in us. If that seed is love, then we develop in love. If that seed is selfishness, then we consistently develop more selfish, sinful habits. Whatever or "whosoever is born of God doth not commit sin; for His seed [remains] in him: and he cannot sin" (1 John 3:9). The word *commit* in this verse has often been misquoted as meaning "habitually committing sin." The Greek is very clear, however, that the word *commit* (*poieō*)[1] refers to a one-time act. The text then would indicate that certain areas of our soul and spirit must not be born of God; these are unconverted. Those unconverted areas then have seeds within them that are "earthly, sensual, [and] devilish" (James 3:15). These seeds will grow selfishness in us.

Jesus said that the second most important commandment is that we are to "love [our] neighbor as [ourselves]" (Matt. 22:39). We just read that men "ought...to love their wives as their own bodies" (Eph. 5:28). We are being challenged to redirect that love of self toward someone else. Instead of selfishly loving ourselves, we need to love somebody else with that same care and concern. This selfless love releases power. The apostle John said that he saw selfless saints overcoming satan because "they loved not their lives unto the death" (Rev. 12:11).

The first and greatest commandment, Jesus said, is similar to the second. We are to "love the Lord thy God with all thy heart, and with all thy soul, and with all thy mind...On these two commandments hang all the law and the prophets" (Matt. 22:37-40). "The law and the prophets" refers to the Scriptures. Jesus is thus saying that without love, none of the aspects of the

Kingdom work. Salvation won't work, deliverance won't work, healing, prophecy, finances, and even relationships won't work without love. Love must be the motivating force for the power and authority in the Scriptures to function. Operating outside of love is to operate in satan's kingdom of darkness.

Sometimes we attempt to operate in both kingdoms at the same time by functioning in duty: doing what is right without the love motive. This is what Scripture calls being *lukewarm*.

When Jeanne and I were first courting, I was working in a city about 50 miles from where she lived. I was saving money for the next semester at the university, but I wanted to do something special for her. I remember driving back after work, and I saw some wild Alberta roses growing in the ditch and decided to pick some. The problem was that Alberta roses grow on very tough and thorny bushes. I had to cut some of the bush in order to have a decent flower, but I had no knife or scissors. All I could find were some rocks, which I used to beat the bush into submission. I got all bloodied from the thorns, and the roses went into total shock with my brutal picking methods, but I got roses for my sweetie. She was very gracious when she accepted the roses (but I noticed they weren't in the vase the next day).

My decision to endure the hassle, trouble, and pain to get Jeanne something special was made out of love not duty. Duty comes out as legalism, which is a "form of godliness, but [denies] the power" (2 Tim. 3:5). It has no power because within legalism there is no belief that love really works. Legalism does not support the belief that I am loved because of who I am, but rather it promotes the idea that what I do (the religious stuff: pray, give, read the Bible, sacrifice, act holy, etc.) determines my worth. Therefore, there is no commitment to the source of that power (God), but rather to works. Often a legalistic or religious spirit attaches itself to this stronghold or mindset. That spirit reinforces the idea that love is not required, only duty. God hates this attitude of duty and pushes us away from Him when we insist on performing in this manner, with no love (see Rev. 3:16). Once we are separated from God, we are separated from the source of power. If we have no intimacy, we have no power.

This is why children have no real power; they are selfish and immature. We are commanded to "in love...grow up into Him in all things, which is the Head, even Christ" (Eph. 4:15). Evil is not always determined just by actions but rather by intent. When a child draws on a wall with his crayons, it is cute—messy but cute. When a 20-year-old puts graffiti on a wall, it is vandalism and a criminal offense.

I was out walking with my friend one day when he leaned over and spit on me. I was none too happy, but he was my friend, so I just brushed it off and continued our walk. We talked until we ran into a group of people I wanted to introduce my friend to. As I was introducing him around, he spit on me again. I would have been upset, but my friend was only one year old! If you can take the attitude that anyone who spits on you is just a baby and is immature, then you too will be able to brush it off and continue to love them. A child is not evil simply because he is immature, but an immature child is selfish.

Immaturity is not a sign of age but rather growth. If we have not grown up, no matter what our age, we are immature, and we will not have much love. The Bible says that faith works (is energized) by love (see Gal. 5:6). If love is the power behind faith then the inverse is true; selfishness is the power behind fear. That makes fear and love mutually exclusive. The Bible says that "perfect love casts out fear" (1 John 4:18). Where there is fear, there cannot be love.

I have ministered to mothers who were very controlling of their children, who flippantly said, "I was afraid they would get into trouble, and I guess I love them too much to let that happen." That actually can't be true. If they are afraid, then because of selfishness, they control their children. It is not love. It is also true that where there is selfishness, there cannot be faith, and thus there cannot be power.

Satan displayed the first selfishness in the universe when he bragged, "I will be like the most High" (Isa. 14:14). He proceeded to bring that selfish, envious attitude into the Garden of Eden. He suggested to Adam and Eve that they also could be like God (see Gen. 3:5). That first act of selfishness resulted in the first fear showing up (see Gen. 3:10). Two opposite progressions have entered the world as a result of Adam's sin:

1. Satan authors selfishness, which spawns fear, which births sin. Sin then manifests as the deeds of the flesh, which are: immorality, impurity, sensuality, idolatry, witchcraft, hatred, strife, jealousy, outbursts of anger, disputes, dissensions, factions, envying,

murders, drunkenness, carousing, and things like these (see Gal. 5:19-21).

2. God authors love, which empowers faith, which is accounted as righteousness. Righteousness, which is by faith, grows "the fruit of the Spirit...[which] is love, joy, peace, patience, kindness, goodness, faithfulness, gentleness, self-control" (Gal. 5:22-23).

The whole reason people develop in selfishness is a vain attempt to gain their own life and liberty. Jeanne has always made it a point to buy birthday gifts for those who don't buy back and are not thankful. Jesus made a point of commanding us to be like Him and to do good, hoping for nothing again, and then we shall be children of the Highest for He is kind unto the unthankful and to the evil (see Luke 6:34-35). It is a way of saying, "You are not able to dictate or manipulate my actions." She chose to respond to the Spirit's love response, and not react to the person's selfishness.

Over the years, we have done the same thing in regard to tithing. We tithed according to the wage we wanted, not according to the wage we received. We diligently did this whenever I had no job. Faith was the proper response to the flesh's fear.

The problem is that selfishness plunges people into the demonic progression, which "through fear of death... [makes them] all their lifetime, subject to bondage" (Heb. 2:15). Real freedom comes from operating in love and giving away our lives in the faith that Jesus has conquered death for us (see Rev. 1:18). Jesus was encouraging us to follow His path, when He said, "Whosoever...shall lose his life shall preserve it" (Luke

17:33). This is the power of the indestructible life. Jesus physically demonstrated that power over His own life through His death and resurrection. He had previously told His disciples that "I have power to lay…[My life] down, and I have power to take it again" (John 10:18). He conquered death by dying and rising again. He challenged His disciples that the only way to gain life and liberty was to die to our own desires and selflessly love others.

Jesus modeled that life through death principle by dying for the Church. His death cleansed the Church and allowed Him to "present it back to Himself a glorious church" (Eph. 5:27). Husbands, if we will lay down our lives (our selfishness) for our wives, we will gain back a respectful, grateful, praise-filled wife as Jesus did.

Jesus said that the greatest love a man could show was to "lay down his life for his friends" (John 15:13). This is why men and women who enter into a battle, whether with guns or in prayer, develop a deep love for each other. David could say of Jonathan, "Thy love to me was wonderful, passing the love of women" (2 Sam. 1:26). When in battle, David and Jonathan had stood in the midst of thousands of men demonstrating their love; they were all laying down their lives for each other. War, of any kind, can be an expression of love rather than hatred and evil. It all depends on the intent of our hearts. Our receiving of love in these circumstances does not depend on our comrades being perfect or even being pleasant toward us. It comes in the demonstration of their love toward us, in their willingness to lay down their lives. Truly "love is the fulfilling of the law" (Rom. 13:10).

Jeanne had a friend who needed deliverance from fear, masturbation, and lust. She had been to many professionals who had not been able to help her. She was a real mess, and her family also was a disaster as a result of her problems. Jeanne was a true friend and spent a lot of time with this lady, literally laying down her life, so that she could be free. It was not Jeanne's great expertise that set her friend free. It was the demonstration of love with no condemnation that had the power over the enemy. Jeanne provided a place where the woman could unlock the events that had spawned her fears. Her parents had once teased her when she was a little girl and had threatened to throw her out of a speeding car. That hidden incident came to life as Jeanne walked her through things. After the lady forgave her parents, she was able to expel the demon of fear that had plagued her for years. The sexual problems were easy to remove after the fear was displaced.

Ministry of any depth will take time and cost you your life. You will get dirty cleaning other people's toilets, and you will have to sacrifice your free time. This laying down of our lives for our friends is one thing, but Jesus wants to take us to an even higher plane of warfare: loving our enemies.

Jesus said, "Love your enemies, bless them that curse you, do good to them that hate you, and pray for them which despitefully use you, and persecute you; that ye may be the children of your Father which is in heaven" (Matt. 5:44-45). If we want to be powerful children of God, we must follow this commandment. Jesus is not asking us to do this; He is commanding us.

Jeanne and I have seen some people who despised us later come to us for counsel because they knew we had the answers that would set them free. Sometimes laying down your life will entail speaking the truth to someone, knowing that it might destroy a friendship. If we do it with the right heart motives, we will please God. The Word says, "When a man's ways please the Lord, He makes even his enemies to be at peace with him" (Prov. 16:7 NKJV).

Those who are selfish look out for themselves and try to get for themselves. That is lust. Lust wants to get; love is always giving. Lust is a product of the flesh and causes:

wars and fightings among you.... [Wars] come...even of your lusts that war in your members. You lust, and have not: you kill, and desire to have, and cannot obtain: you fight and war, yet you have not, because you ask not. You ask, and receive not, because you ask amiss, that you may consume it upon your lusts (James 4:1-3).

Lust usually attracts a spirit that wants to feed off of that lust. I remember an incident of a politician who was a homosexual. He was caught stealing an expensive ring and commented when apprehended, "I don't know what came over me." I thought, *I know what came over you. It was a spirit of lust.* We often don't realize that, when we use demonic structures, such as lust, to gain in one area of our life, we can't dictate where or when that spirit decides to operate; it will dictate. Satan is not opposed to cooperating with you, but he will never be subservient to you. He will always make you his slave.

One of the ways of defeating the lusts that are in our flesh is to always be giving and looking out for the good of others. Jeanne exercised this expression of love by giving away a small inheritance she had received when her father died. Instead of spending the money on herself, she decided to take the entire family, grandchildren and all, on a Mexican vacation. The holiday was a memorial to her father and a method of blessing our children. Love has power to reproduce the blessing we impart to others in our own life.

Abraham wanted a child of his own. God prompted him to intercede for the Philistine kingdom, whose wombs God had closed. Almost immediately Abraham's own wife conceived (see Gen. 20:17–21:2). If we want to have a ministry, we need to sow into somebody else's ministry. Giving will kill the lust of envy and jealousy that is in our flesh. It will also release love in our hearts, empowering faith to grow until it produces what we have been asking God for. There is always power released in exercising love.

The power released in loving is able to drive out our fear. "There is no fear in love; but perfect love casts out fear: because fear hath torment" (1 John 4:18). Where there is love, there is no fear. If there is fear, then there is no love, and selfishness becomes our driving force. A predictable set of responses begins to unfold under this scenario. Because we cannot get our prayers answered, torments start and we cannot find peace. This lack of peace engenders more fear. Fear, powered by our selfishness, precludes the existence of faith, thus preventing our prayers from being answered. We then seek to control what we cannot change, which is the natural response to fear. When we have lost control inside of ourselves (control of our emotions), as indicated by the fear, the torment, and the lack of peace, then we will attempt to control outside of ourselves (our environment and our situations). It becomes a vicious cycle, and only more control seems to be the solution to alleviating our mounting fears. More control creates more selfishness and diminishes our capacity to love. In this selfish state we become "lovers of pleasures more than lovers of God; having a form of godliness, but denying the power" (2 Tim. 3:4-5). The final result is mature selfishness, which has no power.

If we are maturing in love, then the fruit of self-control will be perfected in us. If we are operating in self-control, we will have no fear and will not try to control everything and everyone around us. We need to check ourselves. If we are not comfortable being out of control, then there is an area within us that is selfish, unconverted, and operating in fear. In that area we will have no power and will need healing. The love of a mother for her children empowers her to overcome her natural fears and to rush into a burning building to save them.

Love is more powerful than fear. It drives fear out—not the other way around. Love becomes an action and doesn't just stay as a feeling. Jesus said, "Inasmuch as ye have done it unto one of the least of these My brethren, ye have done it unto Me" (Matt. 25:40). We love the Lord by loving His people and serving them.

Jeanne once ministered at another church's outreach to a male prostitute who had AIDS. He needed love, healing, and forgiveness. She had the grace to set him free, enough to respond to the love of the Lord and receive God's forgiveness and salvation.

I remember doing street ministry at the bars in Guatemala. The men there were trapped in decrepit cantinas, drinking with haggard-looking, toothless prostitutes passed out on their laps. My heart went out to them in their depraved state, and I wanted to show love and compassion. We convinced some of them to come with us to a more conducive place for ministry.

We helped them get up and leave as the other patrons fired off remarks in Spanish that I couldn't understand. They were dead drunk, urinating in the streets and incapable of walking unaided, but we staggered down the street with these guys. As I piled them like cordwood in the back of our little pickup, I questioned God, "Are these the best candidates You can find? They are so drunk; they don't even know what is going on." We drove them back to the House of Refuge and helped them out of the truck.

After plying them with a little coffee, our team started to minister to them. To my surprise, they started crying, throwing up, and repenting. Some healings started as we moved among them, just loving and speaking words of life. We prayed for them through the smell of sweat, urine, booze, and vomit. It was exciting. Every single one of these men gave their hearts to the Lord. I had to repent for my unbelief in the power of God. Sometimes love is even more powerful than faith.

Love doesn't condemn but always comes in the opposite spirit and looks to encourage. Love is patient and kind. Love is not jealous or boastful or proud or rude. Love does not demand its own way. Love is not irritable, and it keeps no record of when it has been wronged. It is never glad about injustice but rejoices whenever the truth wins out. Love never gives up, never loses faith, is always hopeful, and endures through every circumstance. Love will last forever (see 1 Cor. 13:4-8).

We have friends who went through some bad stretches in their marriage. The husband actually cheated on his wife twice. God supplied grace for his wife to forgive both times. She has been an inspiration for Jeanne and me of the persistent power that love has to heal. I can say with joy that her love and Christ conquered his sin and made a way for restitution of their marriage. Love never fails.

Love is a seed, and it must grow if it is going to produce mature fruit. The Bible says, "We love Him, because He first loved us" (1 John 4:19). We know that Jesus loves us because He laid His life down for us and forgave us, but we need to grow in our love. Jesus gives us the key to growing in love in a parable about two men who owed money. One owed a large sum and the other a little. Both had their debt forgiven. Jesus asked a Pharisee, "…Which of them will love…[the] most?" The Pharisee answered, "…He, to whom he forgave most" (Luke 7:42-43). Then Jesus directed His attention toward the prostitute who had prompted the exchange between Him and the Pharisee by washing Jesus' feet and said, "Her sins, which are many, are forgiven; for she loved much: but to whom little is forgiven, the same loves little" (Luke 7:47). To grow in love we must grow in our understanding of how much we have sinned and how much we owe to God.

We must be able to see our sins clearly if we are to properly comprehend our debt. Earlier in my life, I had a hard time repenting because I thought if I did something wrong I would be judged as bad. I had the ridiculous idea that God only found out about my sins if I confessed them. If I kept them hidden, they would not be held against me. However, God knew about my sins before I even committed them. He forgave me as soon as I asked Him, and He was aware of them even before I was. That inability to acknowledge my sins prevented me from developing in love. *Acknowledging sin, our sin, allows us to grow in love.*

God wants us to mature into love like Him. After challenging His disciples to pray for their enemies, Jesus said, "Be ye therefore perfect, even as your Father which is in heaven is perfect" (Matt. 5:48). God actually expects us to be able to think like He thinks and act like He acts because He has fashioned us like His Son (see Rom. 8:29).

Jesus spoke another parable about two men who owed debts that they could not pay. The one who owed a huge sum was likened unto us. Our debt must have been huge; it cost God His Son's life to pay it. There is no price higher than the worth of Jesus. The other man in the parable, who owed a small sum, was likened to those who have offended us. The first servant (us) was forgiven his debt by the king but would not forgive the small debt owed him. The king became angry when he found out and turned the first servant (us) over to tormentors. Jesus said, "So likewise shall My heavenly Father do also unto you, if you from your hearts forgive not every one his brother their trespasses" (Matt. 18:35). We must recognize our massive debt (our sin) if we are to grow in love enough to forgive those who, in retrospect, owe us a pittance of a debt.

Another way we grow our love is by submitting to correction and receiving discipline. Correction always "seems…grievous: nevertheless afterward it yields the peaceable fruit of righteousness" (Heb. 12:11). *Our ability to receive correction is proportional to our ability to trust the one doing the discipline.* God is trying to mature us. If we want to change, then something has to change in us, and usually it is our way of thinking. "If you endure chastening, God deals with you as with sons…that [you] might be [a partaker] of His holiness" (Heb. 12:7,10 NKJV).

I remember an argument that Jeanne and I once had concerning my excessive working habit. She was pleading for us to spend more time together because she wasn't feeling loved. I protested that I was working hard for her and the kids and that she should appreciate what I was doing. My work was my expression of love for them. After she left in frustration, God started to correct me. He said, "You work for yourself not your family. It is not an expression of your love; it is an expression of your ego." I had been spanked. But now, because I knew the truth, I could repent and put my life back in proper order.

If we love others like God loves us, then we will be able to speak the truth in love to these people. Jeanne was ministering to a couple who had gone to a counselor for years yet had not been able to resolve their problems. The wife was so broken, and all attempts to fix her had failed. Jeanne helped her deal with some generational issues, but it was slow going. When

Jeanne got to the sexual part in their ministry, she recognized that they had developed some wrong concepts. The wife had been abused as a young girl and had problems with intimacy. Jeanne helped her through some inner healing and then dealt with the couple's own sexual situations.

Jeanne discovered that because of the wife's former wounds she had a hard time relating to her husband in an intimate manner. To overcome this, they had decided to use pornography as the catalyst before their sexual unions. Jeanne showed them that attempting to use a demonic structure to defeat another demonic structure just drags you further into bondage. This was a revelation for them. Jeanne got them to repent and renounce the use of pornography and to declare their pure love for each other. We received a phone call about a year later thanking Jeanne for her ministry and telling her how they had been set free. Their dependency on pornography to enjoy their marriage relationship had been broken and true love took over. "The truth shall make you free" (John 8:32).

When we are ministering the truth, we must do it in love. God used our experiences with our babies to teach us how to do that. When one of our babies cried at night, wanting a bottle, one of us would get up to feed him. We couldn't just get the formula out of the fridge and fire it into the crib. All that would do is prolong the screaming. We had to pick up the baby, cuddle him, maybe change him and comfort him, until he quieted down. While doing that, we had to warm up the milk until it was just the right temperature. When everything was just right, we could start to feed him. The result was always the same. He would suck back that bottle like he was a vacuum cleaner. Once the feeding was done, the contented baby was burped and rocked back to sleep.

We must treat people the same. The truth (the milk of the Word) must be palatable and served up in love in an acceptable manner. We must always "speak the truth in love…[so they can] grow up into Him" (Eph. 4:15). Because Jesus is the truth and is love, any attempt to communicate the truth outside of love will not manifest Jesus. It will just be a reiteration of the facts and will come out as condemnation. That is the work of the devil and we do not want to participate in his work.

Jesus' purpose in speaking the truth is not to bring condemnation, but rather revelation. He wants us to see where we are compared to where we are destined to be. He wants us to see our selfishness and childishness compared to His love and maturity. Our spirits are designed to be places in which God's Spirit can dwell (see Isa. 66:1), but if we are full of contention and strife, He will not find a resting spot in us. On the other hand, Jesus says, "If anyone loves Me, he will keep My word: and My Father will love him, and We will come unto him and make Our home with him" (John 14:23 NKJV). That is the goal of perfected love.

When Jeanne was a three-year-old, she had an encounter with God. She got up early one morning and went outside just as the sun was coming up. She stood in that sunlight and raised her hands in worship. She had never been to church but just felt the love of the Father flowing over her. God's response to her was a "now expression" of His pleasure in her commitment that she would make 17 years later when she met Jesus. Time is not a limiting factor in the Kingdom. God sees us as what we will become not what we are. He starts the love relationship with us long before the fact of our conversion. Jeanne now understands the truth of what she felt as a little girl. Love always brings revelation.

Satan, on the other hand, blinds. Paul said, "The god of this world hath blinded the minds of them which believe not" (2 Cor. 4:4). Blindness is often manifested as ignorance. For example, I was very independent but thought I was corporate with my wife. The process of becoming one with my wife necessitated the removing of my selfishness. Like all things in the Kingdom, we are not able to change until our fruit, in this case my selfishness, ripens. Once it ripens (becomes obvious), it can be harvested without harming us.

Jeanne and I were taking a mini-vacation to celebrate our 30th wedding anniversary. We were seated together on the plane in one aisle and one middle seat. The row beside us had only one man sitting in the window seat. I slipped over into the other aisle seat across from us and then Jeanne and I had more room and could still talk. I had been working away from home for the last three weeks, and Jeanne and I needed to reconnect. This holiday was going to be a good time for us to just be together.

I started to engage the man I was sitting beside in a conversation, thinking I may be able to witness to him. After the plane lifted off, Jeanne noticed that the row behind me was empty and slipped back into it. The logical move would have been for me to join her so we would have the row to ourselves with lots of room to stretch out. That would have been the logical move, but my independent spirit blinded me. I merrily continued on in my friendly conversation with my new acquaintance until Jeanne slipped me a note. I checked the note. It asked, "What do you think you are doing?"

Suddenly my stupidity struck me. Here I was, on a romantic vacation with my wife, sitting and talking with a stranger while my wife stewed in a seat by herself. I slipped back and humbly began my apologies. Had I more love, I would have seen what was going on without being told.

The more isolated we are, the less loving we become, and the easier it is for the enemy to pick us off. When Israel came out of Egypt, some of the tribes decided to settle outside of the Promised Land because it was "good" for cattle (see Num. 32:1). The farther the Israelites settled from the temple (the presence of God), the sooner they went into captivity (see 2 Kings 10:32-33).

I know a pastor who once had a significant role in the Kingdom. He had been tied into some powerful ministries in the United States and had even represented them overseas. God called him back to Canada where he raised up a lively church. The problem was that he and his wife had a judgmental spirit and had not developed in love. They isolated themselves by only fellowshipping with their congregation as leaders and not as friends. When some of their doctrinal positions were challenged, they could not bring any resolution because they had no love relationships through which they could work things out. They eventually left the church and isolated themselves even further. That developing fruit of selfishness grew in them until they could not fellowship in any church. Even their children, when they grew up, were rejected, and family ties were severed. Without love, we are powerless to see or prevent the plans of the enemy.

Love is the operative force of the Kingdom. Without it nothing works. We can monitor our own progress by seeing how intimate we are with those whom God has entrusted into our realm of authority. If husband and wife are not intimate with each other, they will not be intimate with God. If we do not lay our lives down for those God has entrusted us with, then we are not obeying His commandments. Love always covers; love edifies; love constrains (see Prov. 10:12; 1 Cor. 8:1; 2 Cor. 5:14). If we can't love, we can't function in the Kingdom.

Therefore, if we want to grow in our power and authority, we must:

1. First love ourselves and believe that God loves us.

2. Then we must love others by seeing how much we owe God.

3. Then we can love God.

If we truly love God, we will enter into a covenant with Him to become His "bondservants." In ancient Israel, God set up a system that allowed the Jews to recover from debt without sacrificing their family's inheritance; they could sell themselves as bond slaves for a maximum of seven years. After that they would go free. If the slave loved his master and the family the master gave him, he could bind himself to his new family forever by becoming a bondservant. A bondservant serves his master not out of debt but because of love: "I love my master, my wife, and my children; I will not go out free: Then he shall serve him for ever" (Exod. 21:5-6). In this case, love allowed the bondservant to serve with no need of his own independence.

Today people enter into prenuptial agreements before marriage because, in their minds, they are setting up an exit strategy. That is not love and commitment; that is fear and selfishness. A contract is based on fear and is designed to protect your rights; a covenant is based on love and is designed for you to give away your rights. A contract does not give you power; it gives you leverage. A covenant connects you with the ultimate power in the universe and gives you coverage. "And now abides faith, hope, love, these three; but the greatest of these is love" (1 Cor. 13:13 NKJV).

ENDNOTE

1. Spiros Zodhiates, *The Complete Word Study Dictionary: New Testament* (Chattanooga, TN: AMG Publishers, 1992), #4160 (comp. #4238).

Chapter 8

Forgive and Forget—Forgiveness

Dearly beloved, avenge not yourselves, but rather give place unto wrath: for it is written, Vengeance is Mine; I will repay, [says] the Lord. Therefore if [your] enemy hunger, feed him; if he thirst, give him drink: for in so doing thou shalt heap coals of fire on his head. Be not overcome of evil, but overcome evil with good (Romans 12:19-21).

Forgiveness is the way to peace and perfection. Vigilantes operate where there is no trust in the justice system; they take the law into their own hands. The world and the Church are rampant with vigilantism, and the main forms are by making judgments and holding unforgiveness. Like a vigilante, we become our own judge, jury, and executioner. There can be no mercy because every offense is worthy of instant judgment. Why? Because they are guilty! The problem is: so are we. If we judge others, then we condemn ourselves, "for you who judge practice the same things" (Rom. 2:1 NKJV).

We are all guilty and deserve to go to hell, but God, in His infinite mercy, sent Jesus to die so that through faith in Jesus we might all go to Heaven. Jesus said, "He that is without sin...cast a stone" (John 8:7). If we were perfect, then we, like God, could sit in judgment; but we are not, and Jesus said, "Neither do I condemn you" (John 8:11). If God goes to extraordinary lengths to find a way to forgive people, then we need to find a way to emulate His actions.

We are commanded to love one another (see John 13:34), but we cannot love if we have not forgiven each other. Forgiveness is key to every aspect of the Kingdom. Jesus tied forgiveness into faith when He said,

> ...*Have faith in God.... What things soever ye desire, when ye pray, believe that ye receive them, and ye shall have them. And when ye stand praying, forgive, if ye have aught against any: that your Father also which is in heaven may forgive you your trespasses. But if ye do not forgive, neither will your Father which is in heaven forgive your trespasses* (Mark 11:22,24-26).

There are two requirements listed here to get our prayers answered: pray believing and pray forgiving. God will not listen to prayers that come from an unforgiving heart because He cannot bless us when our character is diametrically opposed to His.

God is more interested in changing us than He is in changing our circumstances. Faith is hearing, believing, and declaring in agreement with God. If we are not forgiving, we cannot come into agreement with God, therefore we have no faith. It is that simple.

When Jesus taught His disciples to pray, He said:

After this manner therefore pray ye: Our Father which art in heaven, Hallowed be Thy name. Thy kingdom come, Thy will be done in earth, as it is in heaven. Give us this day our daily bread. And forgive us our debts, as we forgive our debtors. And lead us not into temptation, but deliver us from evil: For Thine is the kingdom, and the power, and the glory, for ever. Amen (Matthew 6:9-13).

He did not stop there. He went on to say, "For if ye forgive men their trespasses, your heavenly Father will also forgive you: But if ye forgive not men their trespasses, neither will your Father forgive your trespasses" (Matt. 6:14-15). Our salvation depends on us being forgiven, but Jesus links our being forgiven on our willingness to forgive others. I don't think we have realized just how serious God is about this point. We are asking God to forgive us in the same manner that we forgive others. Power to get our prayers answered depends on our willingness to forgive.

The ability for us to even operate in the Spirit depends on our willingness to forgive. The Holy Spirit is very sensitive. He feels all of our pain, hurt, and rejection. That is why He can comfort and console us. He also feels all of our anger, bitterness, and resentment. If we allow these to remain, then we will:

*...grieve...the Holy Spirit of God, whereby ye [we] are
sealed unto the day of redemption. Let all bitterness, and
wrath, and anger, and clamour, and evil speaking, be put
away from you, with all malice: And be...kind one to another, tenderhearted, forgiving one another, even as God
for Christ's sake hath forgiven you* (Ephesians 4:30-32).

The Holy Spirit will not abide with us if we continue to
hold onto our offenses and not forgive those who have wounded
or offended us. If the Spirit in us is grieved by our attitudes and
actions, then we will not have the ability to walk in the Spirit.

We are told that we are to "put on the new man...after the
image of Him that created him [us]" (Col. 3:10). We are to wear
Christ as a garment that covers all of our old nature. God did
this in type for Adam and Eve when He made "coats of skins,
and clothed them" (Gen. 3:21). With this clothing, they were
no longer naked; and in fact, when God looked on them, He
didn't see them; He saw the animals that they were literally
dead in. Now if we are dead "with Christ, we believe that we
shall also live with Him" (Rom. 6:8 NKJV).

How are we to live with these new clothes? "Put on...bowels
of mercies, kindness, humbleness of mind, meekness, longsuffering; forbearing one another, and forgiving one another, if any
man have a quarrel against any: even as Christ forgave you, so
also do ye" (Col. 3:12-13). Part of our garment of Christ is our
ability to forgive anyone who has a quarrel against us. This is
our high calling and is an element of our love walk, putting "on
love, which is the bond of perfection" (Col. 3:14 NKJV).

Some would argue that if we are always forgiving people for everything they do against us that we will just become doormats that others will walk on. In fact the opposite is true. Even psychological research has found that forgiveness is important to "protect…against hatred and resentment that can increase anxiety or depression within oneself, and so forgiveness is in fact a way to protect oneself."[1] Forgiveness is not the same as reconciliation. Forgiveness is one person's stance toward another, while reconciliation requires two people to participate in the process. The forgiver is not blind to the offender's faults but is reducing the negative effects of hatred and resentment.

Peter asked Jesus on two different occasions how much forgiveness he was required to give. Jesus replied, "I say not unto thee, Until seven times: but, Until seventy times seven" (Matt. 18:22). If we use that as a daily guide, then that works out to 490 times a day. That is twice a minute for a 16-hour day or 178,850 times per year. This is important to God, and He does not want us to miss out on the benefits.

While I was writing this, a friend of ours, Sandra, called to thank us for helping her walk through some intercession and forgiveness for her former husband. She said she had never felt so free and happy as she had in the past two days. Her willingness to forgive separated her from the bondages and accusations of the past and allowed her to enter into the future with hope. Forgiveness is freedom and power.

Jesus highlights this aspect of freedom that comes with the forgiveness by a parable that He spoke to Peter right after his question (see Matt. 18:23-35). You may recall that we discussed this same parable earlier, yet it is worthwhile to take another look to see what else we can learn from it. In the parable Jesus tells of a servant who owed approximately $10,000,000 that he could not pay back. The king showed mercy and forgave the debt. This servant promptly went out and grabbed his own servant and demanded that he pay back a $20 debt. When he couldn't, the first servant threw the second into prison. The king was so angry that he brought a judgment upon the first servant and turned him over to the tormentor in prison until the debt was settled. Two results of unforgiveness rear their heads in this parable: getting locked up in a prison and being given over to tormentors.

A prison could be any stronghold that prevents you from moving in freedom. Strongholds are structures in our minds that we create by accepting lies or facts that oppose the truths of the Kingdom (the revealed word of God). These lies are stacked one upon another until they form a stronghold that prevents light (truth) from penetrating into our minds and prevents us from escaping the web of these lies. These negative thoughts put down roots into unhealed areas in our souls and spirits and mature to produce fruit. Negative seeds will produce negative fruit that will destroy our bodies, our minds, and our souls.

Our prisons in our minds will lock us out of all the blessings God intended us to walk in. We will be cut off from family and friends, from health, from prosperity, from joy, and from peace. The first servant had the key to getting both him and the second guy out: all he had to do was to forgive the $20 debt. Jesus likened that little debt to the offenses that others inflict upon us. The $10,000,000 debt would not even compare with the price Jesus paid to set us free. We need to recognize the great mercy that we received if we are to properly judge our lack of mercy in not forgiving others.

The lies of that prison, in which we wall ourselves, are our tormentors. Satan is not our friend. He lies and says that we would be better off protecting ourselves in our own prison and then sends in fear, doubt, depression, anger, bitterness, resentment, revenge, hatred, rage, self-hatred, regret, guilt, condemnation, and many other destructive feelings with which to beat us up.

I was ministering to a gentleman whose wife was acting very rebelliously and bitterly toward him. The Bible says, beware "lest any root of bitterness springing up trouble you, and thereby many be defiled" (Heb. 12:15). That night I had such an attack, in my emotions, against that lady that I had to get up at 4 A.M. and deal with it. I repented for myself, for those areas where I was bitter, rebellious, and judgmental. It was not until I repented for myself and interceded for her that I could chase those tormenting thoughts away. We can't stop birds from flying over our heads, but we can stop them from nesting in our hair. We can't stop demonic attacks, but if we won't come into agreement with them, they can't stay. Solomon said, "….the curse causeless shall not come" (Prov. 26:2). The bitterness in me hooked into the defilement from her and allowed the demonic attack to be effective. Though I had fought and agonized over my feeling all night, as soon as I prayed, they disappeared. I never gave the situation another thought. Those accusations I was fighting were not mine; they were from tormenting spirits that defiled me until I got into prayer to remove them. The only reason they bothered me that long was because I didn't recognize what was attacking me and I hadn't been clean myself when I went into battle.

In the aforementioned parable, the tormentors (see Matt. 18:34) were sent to the first servant because the king withheld his forgiveness. When we refuse to forgive, we will also send and receive tormentors.

Jeanne had firsthand experience with such an attack at a recent conference (prophetic school) that we attended. Six months earlier she had given a prophetic word to a man who visited our church. She gave the word publicly, with our pastor standing right beside her. I was also present in the service as her covering. The word given had to do with the light she saw on him, and she also gave an admonition for him to not judge the church. Jeanne is a very gentle and kind person, and to people not under our covering, she only gives prophetic words that edify, exhort, or comfort. However, the man could only hear the part about not judging. He became offended and never came back to the church.

As it happened, he was doing the registration at the prophetic school and when he saw her name and the others from the church, the very thing that the prophetic word warned him not to do, he did, which was to judge. He ended up under Jeanne in their small group and opposed everything that she suggested. Jeanne did not recognize who he was but could feel the resistance and the judgments. Each night she would come home and express her desire not to return to the school. She would have to pray just to stop feeling the anger and hatred she felt coming against her.

This went on for four days until the last day of school. I was not able to go that last day, so Jeanne reluctantly went without me. That day, this man's wife took Jeanne aside and confronted her with all of their offenses against her. Jeanne could not believe that they, as leaders, would carry these judgments for so long or that they would not have tried to reconcile at the beginning of the school. Jeanne could hardly remember the incident in the church but apologized and repented for causing offense. Jeanne was crying when some of our people came and rescued her from this difficult situation.

The last few hours of the school were designed for the participants to speak prophetic words over each other. Though Jeanne was an emotional wreck at this point, she knew that the enemy was just trying to shut her down. So Jeanne shook off the feelings, forgave the couple for holding onto their anger so long, and started to minister to the others who were present. One of the ladies had a word for Jeanne and wanted the whole school to sing it to her. It was the song, "You are so beautiful to me." God was stating His opinion of how He saw her.

Jeanne went to the man overseeing the school and asked him what the word was that God had given them concerning her. He said that he had heard the word that Jeanne was a prudent woman but that tormentors had been released against her. He asked her if she had dealt with the tormentors. She replied that she had. Later that night we again forgave the couple who had not forgiven Jeanne of the perceived harsh word. After all, if we would not forgive them, we would be cooperating with satan in releasing tormentors against them.

Two events are happening continually before the throne in Heaven. Jesus is continually interceding for us, and satan is continually accusing (see Heb. 7:25; Rev. 12:10). Which one do you want to emulate? Our response should be like Jesus, "The Son can do nothing of Himself, but what He seeth the Father do: for what things soever he doeth, these also doeth the Son likewise" (John 5:19). In other words, whatever the Father does is what the Son does in the same way. If Jesus is interceding for forgiveness, then we should have the same attitude and actions, no matter how we feel.

If we hold unforgiveness and speak accusations against people, we have just entered satan's realm. Whatever sin we were unwilling to forgive pales in comparison to the judgments we are now releasing. Jesus calls us hypocrites if we don't first remove the plank (our judgment) from our own eyes. Then we will see clearly to remove the speck (sin) that is in our brother's eye (see Luke 6:42). Our own peace and the peace of the people we associate with depends on our willingness to forgive and not hold accusations.

Several years ago, I was sitting by myself in the union hall waiting for the meeting to start, when I spotted Ralph (not his real name). He had worked for me about ten years before as the job steward. I had been extremely hard on him when he tried to mediate between the union and myself. At the time I was the superintendent of a construction company. I was very ambitious in those days and prone to pushing through problems no matter who was in the way. Most of the time, on this job, it was Ralph who was in the way. I slipped over beside him and started to talk to him. "Ralph, I want to ask your forgiveness for the way I treated you on the dragline. I was pushy and arrogant and I gave you way more grief than you deserved. I am sorry that I acted that way. Can you forgive me"?

Ralph looked at me in a disdainful way and then said, "No, I will not forgive you. I am still mad at you, and I will never forgive you."

I replied, "I understand your feelings, but I still want to apologize and I am truly sorry for all the pain I caused you." I went back to my seat and waited for the meeting to start. I hadn't thought of Ralph for more than a couple of minutes in the ten years before this incident, and I haven't thought about him since until now when I was looking for a good story to illustrate a point for this book. From conversations related to me, I know that Ralph still holds our conflict close to his heart. The hurts I caused him were painful, but the feelings of resentment are something that he has chosen to hold onto and nurture so that the pain automatically becomes part of his package of offense.

Jeanne and I have discovered that people who nurse a wound for a long period of time actually like the feelings. Ron, a dear friend of ours, had come over for some counsel concerning his feelings of rejection and abandonment. He was expressing how debilitating these feelings were to his relationships and how much he hated them and desired to get rid of them. We had ministered to this same problem many times, and we needed some revelation if we were going to get at the root problem. Suddenly I saw a picture of him holding these hurts close as if he were coddling a baby. He was rocking these wounds back and forth and lovingly feeding them. He didn't hate them; he loved them! That's why he could never get rid of them. The Word says, "to depart from evil is understanding" (Job 28:28), and "the upright is to depart from evil: he that keepth his way preserveth his soul" (Prov. 16:17). *What we don't hate, we will never get rid of.*

Ron had hung onto those hurts and kept them alive by rehearsing them in his mind. Once Ron realized he was coddling and fondling those feelings, he was aghast and immediately repented and rejected them. Thought patterns are pathways that we create in our minds by continually going down those paths. Scientifically they are referred to as neuropath ways, the routes that direct the electrical impulses that make up our thoughts. The more we use the pathways, the more deeply they become entrenched as our default thoughts. The problem is that by continuously traveling these pathways, we put ourselves in harm's way by not forgiving.

There's an old adage that says: holding onto resentment is like taking poison and hoping the other person gets sick. The other one doesn't get sick; you do. Ralph, as he admitted, was still mad at me ten years after the fact; he was in a prison (mentally, emotionally, and perhaps even spiritually). I was free and hadn't even thought about the situation for years. Ralph was not in my mind but, by his own choice, I was in his. How foolish it is to allow a person you hate to occupy a permanent space in your thoughts. *The only way to evict hatred is to forgive.*

Forgiveness is not something we do for the people we are forgiving; it is something we do for ourselves. The other people may get benefits also, but any effort on our part to make them pay for what they have done costs us more than it is worth because of the anger associated with the unforgiveness. Many studies have looked at the link between anger, resentment, and forgiveness as they relate to physical and psychological health:

- One study found that subjects who had a high level of expressed anger experienced significantly higher levels of heart problems, severe personal problems, and poorer general health than those whose character expressed low levels of anger and were more easy going.[2]

- Studies suggest that suppressing your anger is less beneficial than venting it. Researchers found that inhibiting the expression of anger was a larger factor contributing to chronic pain than the expression of that anger or depression.[3]

- Quantitatively, angry men are six times more likely to suffer heart attacks by the age of 55 and three times more likely to develop heart or blood disease.[4]

- Even a single outburst of anger makes men and women two times as likely to suffer a heart attack within the first two hours after such an outburst.[5]

- Strokes are often connected to anger outbursts, as people are 14 times more likely to have a stroke in the first two hours after an outburst of anger.[6]

- Studies have found that the stress and tension that unforgiveness creates is more dangerous to our health than smoking.[7]

Anger and resentment are our enemies. Hanging onto these emotions is detrimental to our physical and mental well-being. The only way to rid ourselves of these forces is to forgive. God expects us to forgive; in fact, He commands us to forgive. John says that "whoever hates his brother is a murderer, and...no murderer has eternal life" (1 John 3:15 NKJV).

Holding resentments has been likened to two people pulling on a rope with resentment as a knot between them. If they keep pulling, that knot may become so tight that it will never come undone. The only way to prevent that from happening is for us to let go of our end of the rope quickly. We don't know what role God has ordained for people to play in relationship to our lives. If we write them off because of offense, we may have just lost the very ones through whom God had planned to bless us.

The apostle Paul is a good example of this principle. He had persecuted the Church and brought untold suffering to many people in his zeal to wipe out the sect he considered heretical. When he was converted, the same murderous spirit was turned against him, and he had to be aided by the very ones he had tried to arrest. These Christians in Damascus had to let Paul (Saul) down by a rope to escape those trying to kill him. Had they not forgiven him, the majority of the New Testament would not have been written.

We receive no reward for loving those who love us or treat us well (see Matt. 5:46). Jesus says that even sinners do that (see Matt. 5:47). We have been called to a higher walk. Jesus calls us to:

Love your enemies, bless them that curse you, do good to them that hate you, and pray for them which despitefully use you, and persecute you; that ye may be the children of your Father which is in heaven: for He maketh His sun to rise on the evil and on the good, and sends rain on the just and on the unjust (Matthew 5:44-45).

That is our command: forgive, pray, and do good to those who hurt us and persecute us. Why? Because that is how God expects His children to respond. Our mandate is to "be...perfect, even as your Father which is in heaven is perfect" (Matt. 5:48). We are called to act out of our spirits and not our souls. We may have every right to resent people for what they have done to us, but Jesus came "not...to condemn the world; but that the world through Him might be saved" (John 3:17).

God has ordained us to be the instruments through whom He accomplishes that:

[Therefore] *put on...as the elect of God, holy and beloved, bowels of mercies, kindness, humbleness of mind, meekness, longsuffering; forbearing one another, and forgiving one another, if any man have a quarrel against any: even as Christ forgave you, so also do ye...And above all these things put on... charity [love], which is the bond of perfectness. And let the peace of God rule in*

*your hearts, to…which also ye are called in one body;
and be…thankful* (Colossians 3:12-15).

Forgiveness—that is what sets us apart from all other peoples on the face of the earth and gives us power and authority to reconcile the world to God.

ENDNOTES

1. Leonard Stampler, "Forgiveness: A Review on a New Trend of Psychological and Medical Research Under Theological Aspects" (Graz: Karl-Franzens-University, 2003).

2. *Journal of Behavioral Medicine*, 10.2 (April 1987), 103-116.

3. *Journal of Behavioral Medicine,* 17.1 (Feb. 1994), 57-67.

4. William J. Cromie, "Anger Can Break Your Heart," *Harvard University Gazette* (Sept. 21, 2006).

5. Ibid.

6. Ibid.

7. Dr. Harold Bloomfield, *Making Peace With Your Past*, WebMD transcript (May 1, 2000), www.webmd.com.

Conclusion

Open the Door to Your Destiny

The day the Israelites entered the Promised Land, Joshua commanded the people to follow the Ark of the Covenant because they had never been that way before (see Josh. 3:4). We too are about to enter our land of promises, and we must follow the new way that the Lord will lead us. *Joshua* in Hebrew is the same as the Greek name *Jesus*; and both Joshua and Jesus led God's people into their promised lands.

By the time the Israelites were ready to enter Canaan, Moses, who represented the covenant of the law, was dead. Under that covenant, Israel had never been able to come out of their selfishness, fear, or slave mentality. Because of their unbelief, God was not able to take them into what He had promised them.

After Moses died, Joshua caused the entire nation to be circumcised at Gilgal. That act "rolled away the reproach of Egypt" (Josh. 5:9) and moved them into liberty. God is calling us to circumcise our hearts: "a circumcision made without hands, in putting off the body of sins of the flesh by the circumcision of Christ" (Col. 2:11).

The old covenant was designed to bring a personal righteousness by following the law. However, human attempts to follow the law, both then and now, deteriorate into legalism, in an effort to maintain that righteousness and holiness. Paul reiterated this concept when he compared the covenant of law versus grace. The law was self effort or flesh and "...persecuted him that was born after the Spirit, even so it is now" (Gal. 4:29). That is why the Pharisees hated Jesus: He was not bound by the law as they were. The new covenant, signified by the removal of the flesh (the developing of a new character), is designed to bring us into a corporate liberty. Self-righteousness is selfishness because it is all about me and my salvation. The new call is to use our liberty to serve others. "For, brethren, ye have been called unto liberty; only use not liberty for an occasion to the flesh, but by love serve one another" (Gal. 5:13).

We are set free so we can love. Our old character, our old way of thinking, was formed in us long before any of us encountered the Lord. Those thought patterns are developed by age three and usually set by age eight. Those patterns were designed to protect us when we were small but become restrictive as we mature in character.

Jesus is calling us to inherit our new destiny, but the old character cannot take us there. The entire army of Israel that left Egypt (their strength) had to die before they could go into the new inheritance. We must also let God kill everything in us that we have relied upon other than Him. That is the key to our victory. God is going to empower His character in us; He will not empower our flesh. This power is for the corporate Body, not for private agendas or personal gain. God's desire is to display His Son to the world through us. That is our calling.

We are going to new heights in the Lord, and only an infusion of His character will be able to sustain us at those heights. It is into His mature character in us that God will pour His Spirit. We all want the power, but not many of us have been willing to go through the process (circumcision of the flesh) to look like Jesus so that we can have it. God is pleased with His Son, and if we want to please God, we must look like His Son.

Rise up! Get ready! The day of the Lord is about to come upon the earth. We are the new creation transformed into the image of Jesus. He has chosen us to be His ambassadors. He has empowered us to walk in power and authority. He wants to dwell in us and live through us. The whole of "the creature [creation] waiteth for the manifestation of the sons of God" (Rom. 8:19). That's us! That's *you*!

Lay hold of the promises, the destinies, and the anointings that God has laid up for you. I hope and pray that you will allow God to mold your character to conform to His, for that is the door to your destiny.

Appendix A

In Chapter 5, I made the statement: "God is always changing the rules as we move higher into His purposes." The Bible says, "Jesus Christ the same yesterday, and to day, and for ever" (Heb. 13:8). This does not mean that God does not change His approach to dealing with us as we change. Just as a parent changes and adapts the rules to grow with their children, so also God institutes different concepts as we mature. The very fact that there is both an Old and New Testament shows that God changes the way we are allowed to approach Him. Jesus came to establish the new covenant, which allowed us to come into God's presence. Hebrews 10:9 states, "...He taketh away the first that He may establish the second." When Jesus died the "veil of the temple was rent in twain from the top to the bottom" (Mark 15:38). This allows us to enter into "the holiest by the blood of Jesus, by a new and living way, ...through the veil, that is to say, His flesh" (Heb. 10:19-20). That was never possible under the Old Covenant. Even the covenant established on the original day of Pentecost (the 50th day after the Sabbath of Passover week, see Leviticus 23:14-15, also called the Feast of Weeks, see Deuteronomy 16:10), which was the giving of the law, was changed when the Holy Spirit was given at the second Pentecost (see Acts 2). This changed was foreshadowed when Jeremiah prophesied:

> *Behold, the days come, saith the Lord, that I will make a new covenant with the house of Israel, and with the house of Judah: not according to the covenant that I made with their fathers... which my covenant they brake.... But this shall be the covenant that I will make.... After those days...I will put my law in their inward parts, and write it on their hearts; and will be their God and they shall be My people* (Jeremiah 31:31-33).

God has always wanted to do that; He never changed, but the rules did.

Appendix B

In Chapter 6 I raised the question, can a Christian have a demon? That is a controversial question. From personal experience and hundreds of ministry sessions, the answer is a definitive, yes! We are not talking demon possession, which indicates being under the power of a demon.[1] Rather, I am talking about a state where a demon has access to an area of our souls and can make a claim to stay there because that area is not submitted to Christ. Jesus said, "...the prince of this world cometh, and hath nothing in me" (John 14:30). There was no place or thing in Jesus that a demon could control because all areas were yielded to the Father. We are not way. John wrote, "If we say that we have no sin,...the truth is not in us" (1 John 1:8). Later in the same book, he made a dramatic statement when he said, "Whosoever is born of God doth not commit sin; for His seed remaineth in him: and he cannot sin, because he is born of God" (1 John 3:9). These two verses would seem to be mutually exclusive unless we examine the meanings of the words. *Whosoever* could just as easily been translated "whatsoever" or "all things,"[2] as it was in John 1:3 ("All things were made by Him...").

If I am born of God and I still sin, which I do, then it follows that there must be places within me that are not born of God or are unconverted because in the converted areas I cannot sin. Jesus used this term *converted* often (see John 12:40, Luke 22:32, Matt.18:3) to mean "to turn,"[3] or to change the way we think. The picture here is that we have unconverted areas in or souls where the seed or word of God has not penetrated and where we do not agree with what the word says. In those areas, we are blind and have believed a lie. In those places, satan is able to perpetuate the lie and to put his hooks in us and control how we think because the foundation in that area is based on a lie, which is often the result of a wound. Satan uses his demons to control because, unlike God, he is not omnipresent nor omniscient. The size of the lie or the wound will determine how much control he is able to exercise. Simon the sorcerer (see Acts 8:9-24) in Samaria believed and was converted and baptized in the revival that occurred there. However his response to the outpouring of the Spirit uncovered an area concerning his lust for power and his misconceptions of how the Kingdom operated. Peter said to him, "...Thy heart is not right in the sight of God. Repent [think differently[4]]...of this wickedness...perhaps the thought of thine heart may be forgiven....for I perceive that thou art in the gall of bitterness, and the bond of iniquity" (Acts 8:21-23). Simon was bound up and controlled because he had let a wound make him bitter and cloud his thinking. Once we repent, we can take our authority and demand that the demonic influence that is controlling any realm of our soul is removed.

When we receive the Lord, His Spirit takes up residence in our spirits. Our souls, at this point, have yet to be sanctified and occupied by Him, as is evidence by our continuation of sin. Many of the rooms of this realm can still be controlled and influenced by the demonic. Even satan himself still has access to the throne room of God (see Job 1:6-12). It should be no surprise that he has access to us in those places where we have not allowed God's control. A good book on this concept is *Thrones of Our Soul*, by Paul Keith Davis (Creation House Press, 2003).

Paul, the apostle, said, "In a great house there are...vessels, ...some to honour and some to dishonour. If a man therefore purge himself from these, he sall be a vessel unto honour, sanctified, and meet for the Master's use..." (2 Tim. 2:20-21). This was the war he was talking about when he said, "...when I would do good, evil is present with me. ...I see another law in my members, warring against the law of my mind, and bringing me into captivity to the law of sin which is in my members" (Rom. 7:21,23). He went on to say that within himself he served both God and sin (see Rom. 7:25). We overcome this problem of sin and its bondages by walking in the Spirit: "...for the law of the Spirit of life in Christ Jesus hath made me free from the law of sin and death" (Rom 8:2). This is why self deliverance is so powerful. When we yield, through faith, any area of our life to Christ, all others with claims must withdraw.

ENDNOTES

1. Spiros Zodhiates, *The Complete Word Study Old Testament*, (Chattanooga, TN: AMG Publishers, 1992), #1139.

2. Ibid., #3956.

3. Ibid., #1994.

4. Ibid., #3340.

Treasure Chest Ministries

www.treasurechestministries.ca

MINISTRY CONTACT:

Brenda G. Smith
Treasure Chest Ministries
Box 3458, 180 Century Road
Spruce Grove, AB T7X 3A7

E-mail: brenda@watchman.ca

WORKSHOPS/SEMINARS:

- Breaking Generational Curses and Enacting Your Blessings

- Breaking Judgments and Vows
- Stirring up the Prophetic

RESOURCES:

Please visit the following Website
for available teaching resources:

www.watchman.ca